AW WITH WORDS

Young Writers' 16th Annual Poetry Competition

It is feeling and force of imagination that make us eloquent.

How can I not dream while writing? The blank page gives a right to dream.

Poems From Kent
Edited by Mark Richardson

 Young**Writers**

First published in Great Britain in 2007 by:
Young Writers
Remus House
Coltsfoot Drive
Peterborough
PE2 9JX
Telephone: 01733 890066
Website: www.youngwriters.co.uk

SB ISBN 978-1 84602 804 5

Foreword

This year, the Young Writers' *Away With Words* competition proudly presents a showcase of the best poetic talent selected from thousands of up-and-coming writers nationwide.

Young Writers was established in 1991 to promote the reading and writing of poetry within schools and to the young of today. Our books nurture and inspire confidence in the ability of young writers and provide a snapshot of poems written in schools and at home by budding poets of the future.

The thought, effort, imagination and hard work put into each poem impressed us all and the task of selecting poems was a difficult but nevertheless enjoyable experience.

We hope you are as pleased as we are with the final selection and that you and your family continue to be entertained with *Away With Words Poems From Kent* for many years to come.

Contents

Alex Russell (13)   18
Nicolle Waterton (13)   19
Georgia Elliott (13)   19
Lynsey Stephens (14)   20
Casey Smith (13)   20
Kareen Brown (13)   21

Borden Grammar School
Jagroup Cheema (13)   21
Tom Kennison (13)   22
Chester Field (14)   22
Matt Cavender (13)   23
Alex Shaxted (13)   23
Emile Carstens (13)   24
Jordan Arthurs (13)   24
Mitchell Payne (13)   25
Mark Cryer (13)   25
Lewis Wilde (13)   26
Samuel Johnston (14)   26
Damian Kelly (15)   27
Samuel Collins (14)   27
Jamie Martin (13)   28
Charlie Bowling (13)   29
Andrew Taylor (13)   30
Mitchell Prentice (13)   31
Daniel Gebbie (14)   32
Jack Matthews (13)   32
Conrad Fry (13)   33
Jake Marshall (13)   33
Beau August (14)   34
Jackson Shaddick (14)   35
Michael Barton (15)   35
Tommy Chapman (13)   36
Daniel Glazier (14)   37
Michael Wood (14)   38
Michael Camber (13)   39
Adam Pilfold Bagwell (13)   40

Chatham Grammar School for Girls
Kylie Newport (17)   41

East Court School for Dyslexia

Looch Trevor (12)	42
Petrok Lawrence (11)	42
Jack Walker (12)	43
Luke Lennard (11)	43
Richard Atkins (12)	44
James Hawkins (13)	45
Giles Sparkes (12)	46
Bethany Parrott (11)	47
Edmund Robinson (12)	47

Folkestone School for Girls

Kayleigh Vidler (12)	48
Miriam Tresh (16)	49
Laura Logan (16)	50
Vicki White (16)	50
Joelle Wade (11)	51
Sarah Beech (11)	51
Jennifer Towell (15)	52
Brinsha Rai (11)	52
Natasha Sleeman (12)	53
Abbie Sims (16)	53
Shannon Petrie (11)	54
Rachel Thomas (16)	54
Lauran Jarvis (13)	55
Alexis Noonan (11)	55
Stephanie Mackenzie (16)	56
Danielle Thorpe-Gray (16)	57
Aimee Irving (12)	57
Laura Winstanley (16)	58
Ellie Carter-Leay (11)	58
Victoria Castle (15)	59
Jessica Maynard (11)	59
Madeleine Ubee (11)	60
Hannah Dinnage (11)	60
Sanjidah Islam (11)	61
Ruby McCaffrey (11)	62
Kiera Ward (11)	63
Ruth Wilkie (14)	64

Fort Pitt Grammar School for Girls

Jessica Park (12)	65
Reanna Walters (11)	65
Elena Smitherman (11)	66
Hannah Smith (11)	66
Sammi-Jo Ferigan (11)	67
Emma Gifford (11)	68
Zoe Bartlett (11)	68
Jennifer Woolgrove (12)	69
Kimberley McGee (11)	69
Lucy Smith (11)	70
Corrinne Piper (11)	70
Ayesha Chouglay (11)	71
Emily Light (11)	72
Tiffany Coller (12)	73
India Gillan (11)	74
Hannah Stanford (12)	75
Sophie Hatherly (11)	76
Elizabeth Early (11)	77
Aimee Martin (11)	78
Rebecca Helm (11)	79
Karisma Sathi (11)	79
Charlotte Deeley (11)	80
Guvandeep Dio (12)	80
Rebecca Harpum (12)	81
Liberty Duvall (12)	81
Grace Bell (12)	82
Rhiannon Pike (11)	82
Amy Tibbles (11)	83
Samantha Rankin (12)	83
Bethany Cownden (12)	84
Rianne Hall (12)	84
Helen Kinney (12)	85
Jessica Jagpal (11)	85
Lucy Attwell (11)	86
Louise Campbell (11)	86
Helen Day (11)	87
Abigail Douglas (11)	87
Cloe Jolley (12)	88
Louise O'Leary (11)	89
Emily Heasman (12)	90

Kellie Gadd (11)	90
Linda Hammoum (13)	91
Chelsea Arnold (11)	91
Gabriella Bossman (13)	92
Naomi Latham (11)	92
Sian Varrall (12)	93
Soriah Williams (11)	93
Daisy Counsell (12)	94
Rosie Jarvis (11)	94
Aimee Mills (12)	95
Emily Martin (11)	95
Jordan Turner (12)	96
Kelsey Honess (12)	97
Shannon Arnold (11)	98
Sahel Athari (13)	99
Megan Beard (11)	100
Paige Varrall (11)	101
Eleanor Camber (12)	101
Natasha Scanlon (11)	102
Hannah Goldsmith (11)	102
Emily McCaw (11)	103
Amber Wright (11)	103
Lyndsey Piper (11)	104
Ore Soyinka (11)	105
Paige Arnold (13)	106
Anna Saffery (11)	106
Caroline Prentice (11)	107
Hayley Bowes (11)	107
April Taylor (11)	108
Stacey Owens (11)	108
Emma Webster (12)	109
Brontie Stears (11)	109
Melanie Jones (12)	110
Angela Wright (12)	111
Simran Kaur (11)	112
Stacey Williams (11)	112
Hannah Winterman (11)	113
Rebecca Ansell (12)	113
Amie Turner (12)	114
Katie Gray (12)	115
Louise Hughes (12)	116
Rebecca Cutting (11)	117

Greenacre School

The Poems

Thunderstorm

Clashing through the sky at 100mph,
A beam of purple light
And then a heavy shower,
Flash, flash, bang, bang,
The world is up in lights.

A flicker of blue,
A long streak of red,
Both as deadly as something bad said,
Hits the pavement, hits the sea,
People lose lives tragically.

For who can stop this mighty beast,
This multicoloured death machine?
No one can, not even God,
Whoever that may be.

This is a thing that can't be stopped!

But what creates this thing that makes us scream?
God, you may ask.
There is no right or wrong answer.
    Cold,
        Windy,
            Black,
                Silence.

Jordan Marie Taylor (11)
Archers Court Maths & Computing College

Eeyore

E nchanted heart to love and care,
E ndless love,
Y oung and sweet,
O pen and thoughtful to all his friends,
R aving kindness to share with all,
E ndless hugs.

Lucy Smale (11)
Archers Court Maths & Computing College

Arctic

The Arctic is so cold,
The winter is rather bold.
The Narwhals are jousting,
While the larger whales are shouting.
The seals have had their pups,
The mother's milk they suck.
The polar bear's waiting for a kill,
Thinking of a dead seal doesn't make him chill.
Killer whales with their towering fins,
In a fight, the pod always wins,
The humpback whales have come to breed,
With their massive mouths open they feed.
The harp seals are hunting eels,
The cold, thanks to blubber, none of them feels.
Beluga whales are white as snow,
Although babies are grey, so they show.
Although bitter and blustery,
The Arctic is busy and has a wildlife industry.

Samantha Lucock (11)
Archers Court Maths & Computing College

Winter Seasons

Snow, snow all around,
Like a big white blanket on the ground.
Lots of children having fun,
Throwing snowballs at everyone.

Robin redbreast sings from a tree,
Children shouting with lots of glee,
Once again the time is here
For seasonal spirit and good cheer.

Rhys Iverson (11)
Archers Court Maths & Computing College

Race Horse

Muzzles as smooth as polished wood,
Hooves like curved rocks.
Manes as wild as the wind,
Coats as soft as silk,
Paces slow and fast, like going
Through a time machine,
Tails like long guitar strings.
Perfect leaps over jumps
As if he is jumping a lake.
The course is against the clock.
      Leap,
          Stumble,
              Silence.

Megan Kathleen Saltmer (11)
Archers Court Maths & Computing College

Fruits

An apple, orange and plum,
A hand of bananas sucking its thumb,
Dots on an orange and stripes and splodges on an apple,
Most have a smooth or rough skin,
But mouldy ones go in the bin.
Core in an apple and pips in an orange,
Apples are crunchy,
Pears are munchy,
Plums are smooth and soft to touch,
These are your 5-a-day
And they lead you on your way!

Amber Sayer (11)
Archers Court Maths & Computing College

Wrong

Waking up one fine day
Only to earn my pay.
Come back home,
All alone,
Walk to the cupboard to get some food,
Then I find my mum in a bad mood.
I go to get in the car,
When I remember our drive is covered in tar.
Get to school very late,
When I remember I have not got a mate.
First lesson is maths, I like maths,
When I find I have to sit next to Kath.
I hope my day will get better,
Then my teacher gives me a letter.

Joe Reeves (11)
Archers Court Maths & Computing College

Tiger!

Tiger, tiger, eyes so bright,
In the jungle of the night.
Orange fur, fiery like the sun
Oh, how quickly you can run.

Tiger, tiger, eyes so bright,
In the jungle of the night,
Ever so quietly you do growl
As you silently creep and prowl.

Tiger, tiger, eyes so bright,
In the jungle of the night,
You don't hunt in a pride,
Your prey has nowhere it can hide.

Mollie Foster (11)
Archers Court Maths & Computing College

Football

The grass is green,
The referee is mean,
Someone gets fouled,
Substitution is made.
A player shoots
And off come his boots.
Streaker runs about on the pitch,
Player smashes the ball into the crowd.
That ball is mine,
Burgers and chips at half-time.
Now they have a penalty shootout
And the fans start to shout.
Time to go home
And the losers start to moan.

Kyle Poole (12)
Archers Court Maths & Computing College

Autumn

Autumn time brings lots of fun,
Hello to more cloud and goodbye to the sun.
Conkers and berries appear on the trees,
Lots of people are beginning to sneeze.
Hallowe'en is near, you may get a fright,
The following week is Bonfire Night,
With lots of flames and sparkles around,
Tomorrow empty fireworks you'll find on the ground.
Winter is near, but don't feel down,
Put a smile on your face, not a frown.
The snow will be here soon enough
And so will Christmas, so don't be in a huff.

Jordan Meadows (12)
Archers Court Maths & Computing College

Be All And End All

I can see his lips moving,
Something to do with problem solving,
Daydreaming about the match on Saturday and Sunday,
5, 4, 3, 2, 1, that's the end of the week, hooray!
There is a huge wave of kids all rushing to leave,
It looks like someone has just opened the lid,
What, where and how will I play?
Ooh, did I get homework for Monday?
Not going to worry too much just now,
This is what my life is about,
Football, my life and impressing the scout.
When is your homework due in?
I promise I'll do it tomorrow, I try not to grin.
We gave them the biggest thrashing they ever had,
Mum, Dad and the manager were really glad.
When we got home, the mood seemed somewhat different,
I wished I had paid more attention and listened.
Football is not the be all and end all, Dad would say.
Do you think I will play for Spurs some day?
Pay attention at school, football is not the be all,
I must remember not to daydream when I'm at school.
If I could learn to read Teacher's lips that would help,
Everyone is in bed and Mum and Dad won't help.

Sam Pritchard (11)
Archers Court Maths & Computing College

Winter Season

The hills covered with white snow,
Like a blanket, full of white feathers.
Trees with no leaves, just white wool,
Bare trees still standing tall.
Crystal, magical, slushy snow,
Bouncing off people's houses,
Hugging the path as if in bed,
The falling snow dropping dead.

Ashley Fletcher (11)
Archers Court Maths & Computing College

Why Do Animals Do What They Do?

Why do cats purr and dogs bark?
Why do donkeys kick and
Owls come out in the dark?

Why do hyenas laugh or birds fly high in the sky?
Why do mice squeak and horses sigh?

Why do monkeys eat bananas and tigers roar?
Why do dolphins jump for joy and
Why do eagles soar?

Why do panthers play hide-and-seek and
Why do squirrels collect their nuts?
Why do hippos lie in mud and some animals sniff each other's butts?

So many questions,
So little time,
I hope you enjoyed
My little rhyme.

Bethany Meares (11)
Archers Court Maths & Computing College

Christmas Is . . .

Christmas is a day of fun,
It is when Jesus begun.
Christmas is nothing without snow,
Christmas is all on the go.
Christmas dinner is so nice,
Add some gravy, then some spice.
Christmas with a turkey roast,
My mum makes it best, she always boasts.
Christmas with presents and family,
Christmas is a special day.
It's time for bed now,
Tomorrow's Christmas Day.

Declan Groombridge (11)
Archers Court Maths & Computing College

Ice Skates

When you're on the ice rink you feel you're in Heaven,
With anxious thoughts and happiness.
You feel peaceful, yet scared of falling over.
Small, yet sharp blades can take you for miles.
Sometimes you feel like you may never be able to stop.
When you are ice skating you feel like you can dance
In a circle, round and round until you stop and feel dizzy.
It's like a famous ice skaters' playground and
Where they go to relax and calm down.
It's your chance to shine and dazzle on the ring of ice.
The ice looks like a sheet of glass.
You glide and slither through the ice.

Rebekah Clark (11)
Archers Court Maths & Computing College

My Mum

She is a glittery chandelier,
She is as happy as a dolphin jumping in the sea,
She is a magpie that loves shiny things,
She is a beautiful red rose waiting to be picked,
She sounds like a harp being played by an angel,
She is a roast dinner steaming away,
She is a hot chocolate for when you're upset,
She is a person that likes nature.

Charlotte Fagg (12)
Archers Court Maths & Computing College

My Dog, Gypsy

A bundle of joy,
A sweet sound to our ears,
A sour scent of dog shampoo,
A loveable dog,
A part of my family,
Cute!
Cuddly!
Friendly!

Karlie Clubb (11)
Archers Court Maths & Computing College

Lonely Child

She hit me again,
Purple face, bloody lips,
Tear-stained shirt,
Everyone will ask why.
'What happened?' they'll say.
I'll just run away again.

Got yelled at today,
Abusive language, hurtful comments,
Why does she do it?
What did I ever do?
I'll think about it.
I have no idea.

Work torn to shreds,
Made-up excuse; detention forever,
I couldn't tell Miss the truth.
If I did, social services would be round.
They always get their way
And I don't like care homes.

Alice Lawlor (12)
Ashford Senior School

Through The Eyes Of A Child In The War

Another birth,
Another light,
Hope,
Another night.

Another drop,
Another crust,
Hunger,
Another dusk.

Another time,
Another way,
Fear,
Another day.

Another tear,
Another war,
Anguish,
Another dawn.

Another scream,
Another flower,
Sorrow,
Another hour.

Another grain,
Another voice,
Disease,
Another choice.

Another cry,
Another breath,
Silence,
Another death.

Liza Malby-Hatcher (12)
Ashford Senior School

Memories

I remember,
We packed up our lunch and drove off in the car.

I remember
We arrived and jumped out and ran,
Sand flying beneath our feet.

I remember
We splashed and played,
Daring the waves to come and wet us.

I remember
When the tide went out, we played ball,
Dug holes and made sandcastles.

I remember
My sister, my mum and my dad,
All with smiles on their faces.

I remember
Grinning from ear to ear, I reclined like a hermit in its shell
Behind the dunes.

I remember
It got cold and we were getting ready to go.

I remember
My ears still to this day hear the quietness of the empty space,
Just the sound of the water's waves getting softer.

I remember
They got softer, quieter, softer, quieter,
Softer until the air was cool and silent and all was quiet.

Imogen Ford (12)
Ashford Senior School

Going Back In Time

The room's all clogged up with steam
And all the engines puffing away,
The brass and copper polished clean,
Loud noises and little space.
All the trains running at a slow pace,
Beams of light shining through the glass,
Darker and darker as the sun will pass.

Another explosion with a life,
The steam so thick and grey
You could cut it with a knife,
The sound of metal screeching, being cut,
Coal shovelled in, then the engine door slams shut.
Sometimes I wish I could escape the noise,
But then I fear for the safety of the younger boys.

Through the darkness, noise and grime,
I dream of a land
With air so clear and fine.
The train rattles down the track,
The faces at the windows smiling back.
A one-way ticket to ride my dreams,
Away from this dirt to blue skies and the sea.

Amy Lillington (12)
Ashford Senior School

Friends

My friends are always there for me,
I like it when they come to tea.
It's fun playing at school,
I wouldn't get rid of my friends, not at all.
All the girls are just so cool,
And the boys, so my class rules.
Going to town with my friends,
They're always in the newest trends.
I wouldn't get rid of my friends, not at all,
Not my friends because they just rule!

Nicholas O'Doherty (12)
Ashford Senior School

The Seasons Which I Cannot See

I have never seen the spring,
But the sound of the lambs and
The rustle of the blossom trees is music to my ears.
I can smell the sweet apple blossom.
All of these smells and sounds make up a picture
Which I cannot see.

I have never seen the summer,
The smell of sea salt and the sea was Heaven.
I could feel the sand and the shells beneath my feet.
The sound of the waves and the gulls enabled me to picture
The beach which I cannot see.

I have never seen the autumn,
The sound of the leaves crunching beneath my feet and
The rustle of the trees in the wind makes me feel cool and calm.
The smell of the tree bark and the leaves that I touch make me sense
The maple grove which I cannot see.

I have never seen the winter,
I can feel the cold air making my hands numb
And the bitter wind on my face.
I can taste the snow as it falls on my tongue.
All of these things enable me to feel the snow
Which I cannot see.

Katherine Peart (12)
Ashford Senior School

Eight Things Found In A Dragon's Pocket

A fair maiden,
A bottle of steam,
A bag of fire nuts,
The London Eye,
A spare boiler,
A haunted castle,
Frogs' bones,
And a sun to heat up the sky.

Edward Millgate (9)
Ashgrove School

I'm Somebody!

(A parody of Emily Dickinson's poem 'I'm Nobody')

I'm somebody! Who are you?
Answer me, I don't have a clue.
There's only one of me,
It's been advertised, you know.

How awful to be a nobody,
How dull, like drying paint.
To be unknown to everyone,
It's enough to make you faint!

Sarah Louise Elizabeth Hall (13)
Beaverwood School for Girls

I Am Nobody, Who Are You?

(A parody of Emily Dickinson's poem 'I'm Nobody')

We're all nobodies - who cares?
Are you all nobodies too?
Who cares about being noticed?
It doesn't really matter, does it?

It would be horrible to be somebody,
How noticeable! Like a dragon!
There are so many nobodies,
It would be weird if I was somebody!

Hollie Hughes (13)
Beaverwood School for Girls

Somebody

(A parody of Emily Dickinson's poem 'I'm Nobody')

We're all somebody! Don't you know?
Have you realised you're somebody too?
Then it's official, we're all one group,
We all know who we are!

How dreary to be a nobody!
How reclusive, like a mouse,
To think you're not worth a thing,
Staying alone in your house!

Zainab Malik (13)
Beaverwood School for Girls

I'm Somebody

(A parody of Emily Dickinson's poem 'I'm Nobody')

I'm somebody! Who are you?
Are you nobody, worthless and blue?
Ah! Then we're different, isn't that true?
I'm rich and famous - what about you?

How dreadful to be nobody!
So common, like a name?
A life full of boredom and drear.
Missing the glamour and fame.

Pooja Milhotra (13)
Beaverwood School for Girls

I'm A Nobody, You're A Nobody

(A parody of Emily Dickinson's poem 'I'm Nobody')

I'm a nobody, you're a nobody,
Are you? You are.
Don't tell, I promise, they'd advertise!

It's boring to be a someone, all the same,
You're right about that;
To tell my name
Is to tell your name to a stranger.
Do you know why?

Lola Stanford (13)
Beaverwood School for Girls

I'm Kirsty, Who Are You?

(A parody of Emily Dickinson's poem 'I'm Nobody')

I'm Kirsty! Who are you?
I hope you are Kirsty too!
There's lots of pairs like us.
Do tell, then they'd advertise us.

How boring to not be somebody!
How dull, like a frog.
I hope you're somebody,
Unlike a smelly dog!

Kirsty Beckley (13)
Beaverwood School for Girls

I'm Somebody, Who Are You?

(A parody of Emily Dickinson's poem 'I'm Nobody')

I'm somebody! Who are you?
Are you somebody too?
We can both be somebody!
I don't know any nobodies.

How boring to be a nobody!
How invisible, are you like a speck of bacteria,
For no one to know your name?
Popular you are not,
I think you've lost the plot!

Cheri Randell (13)
Beaverwood School for Girls

We're Somebodies, Who Are They?

(A parody of Emily Dickinson's poem 'I'm Nobody')

We're somebodies, who are they?
Are they somebodies too?
Then there are a few more of us!
Shall we see? But don't make it obvious!

How weird for there to be more of us!
Is it going to be made public?
Wonder what their names are?
It's fantastic to be someone!

Stephanie Grace (13)
Beaverwood School for Girls

I Am Nobody! Who Are You?
(A parody of Emily Dickinson's poem 'I'm Nobody')

I'm nobody! Who are you?
Are you one of those somebodies?
I have no clue.
You may sit unaccompanied like me all day,
Or you may go out and have fun and play.

How boring my life may seem,
So dull and dreary, like a goldfish.
For my name to be recognised
Would be my one and only wish!

Abbie Sargent (13)
Beaverwood School for Girls

I'm Somebody! Who Are You?
(A parody of Emily Dickinson's poem 'I'm Nobody')

I'm somebody! Who are you?
Are you all somebody too?
Really? Then there is a group of us!
Shh, don't tell!

How sad it is to be a nobody,
How wonderful it is to be a celebrity.
All those nobodies - miserable frogs
Sitting in their dreary bogs.

Alex Russell (13)
Beaverwood School for Girls

Young Writers - Away With Words Poems From Kent

I'm Somebody! Who Are You?

(A parody of Emily Dickinson's poem 'I'm Nobody')

I'm a somebody! Who are you?
Good, you're a somebody too!
Then there's a pair of us!
I like being a somebody, everyone makes a fuss.

It must be dreary to be a nobody,
How wonderful it is to be public, like a lion in a zoo!
I love to tell my name
And to be surrounded in fame!

Nicolle Waterton (13)
Beaverwood School for Girls

I Am Somebody, Who Are You?

(A parody of Emily Dickinson's poem 'I'm Nobody')

I'm somebody!
Who do you think you are?
I know you're not a somebody!
I will tell them to get you!

How stupid to be nobody!
How strange, hiding away like a mole!
It is better to be
In the fame game!

Georgia Elliott (13)
Beaverwood School for Girls

I'm Somebody, Who Are You?

(A parody of Emily Dickinson's poem 'I'm Nobody')

I'm somebody, who are you?
Are you somebody too?
Then there is a pair of us!
If you're nobody, then you'd better
Try to be somebody.

How lonely to be nobody!
How public, like a fox!
I love to hear my name,
All covered in a frame!

Lynsey Stephens (14)
Beaverwood School for Girls

I'm Casey, Who Are You?

(A parody of Emily Dickinson's poem 'I'm Nobody')

I'm Casey! Who are you?
Are you Casey too?
Then there are two of us!
Don't tell, they will advertise, you know!

How dreary to be nobody,
How horribly private!
Like a horrid, dim snail!

Casey Smith (13)
Beaverwood School for Girls

I'm Nobody! Who Are You?

(A parody of Emily Dickinson's poem 'I'm Nobody')

I'm somebody! Who are you?
Are you somebody too?
Then there's a pair of us, right?
Come on tell, they'd advertise you know!
We'll be famous, you'll see,
We'll be on talk shows, you and me!

How great to be somebody!
How public, like a shark,
To tell one's name the live-long June
To an admiring sea!

Kareen Brown (13)
Beaverwood School for Girls

Trees

Trees, trees, why do they bother us?
Can't they see we are over that?
Five-year-olds screaming with fuss,
Parents losing all of their fat.
Why are they brown and green?
Were they meant to be red and pink?
They are a good screen,
But they can shrink.
We have gone to all this trouble
Helping to grow and mature these plants.
Now they have grown double
And we can all chant.

Jagroup Cheema (13)
Borden Grammar School

Florida

We sat down in our seat
Wondering which fate we would meet

People came to check my belt
But they didn't know how I felt

I didn't know what would happen
Wondering about riding the 'Kraken'

Then we went up and down, round and round
And even went underground

We went up, up so high
I thought I could touch the sky

People shrieked with fear
As the ride plummeted down in top gear

The ride stopped with a jolt
As we felt all shook up to a pulp

Ten out of ten I would rate
As Florida is the sunshine state.

Tom Kennison (13)
Borden Grammar School

The Dog

His name is Fred,
His fur is browny red.
He has floppy ears
And teeth like spears.
He barks really loud,
But it's a very weird sound.
He snuggles down deep
In his fluffy bed when he falls asleep.
His breed is a pug,
He looks like a cute bug.
He is very small,
Only fifteen centimetres tall.

Chester Field (14)
Borden Grammar School

Belief

In a world where everyone is unique,
Where everyone has an opinion,
Where everyone has a belief,

Where religions bring out the best in people,
Something that makes us unique,
Something that makes us different,

But the thing that makes us unique
Will sometimes tear us apart,
Will cause death and conflict in the world.

Lots of innocents dying,
War breaking out over the world,
But this is the thing that makes our planet,

The thing that makes our world
Interesting, fun and different.

Matt Cavender (13)
Borden Grammar School

Fire

The fire crackles in the hearth,
Fire gives the heat that warms you,
Blazing brilliantly for all to see,
Fire gives the light that surrounds you,
The primitive central heating.
Fire gives the warmth that goes down to your toes,
Stimulating the room.
Suddenly it is extinguished,
It gives out its heat no more.
No longer will its light surround us,
No longer will our toes be warm,
Not until it is re-lit, tomorrow at dawn.

Alex Shaxted (13)
Borden Grammar School

My Dove

Under a tree sat a lonely sight,
Awaiting nature to have her way,
Soon to be killed by the cold of night,
Gone with the wind at the break of day.
But he would have the chance of the year,
A second chance to save his life.
As I went closer, he was in fear,
I picked him up to prevent strife.
My grandad said he was a dove,
I took his word and made him a house.
'When he is older he would find love.'
Months passed and he made friends with my mouse,
Soon after, he lost his baby down.
I started to help him learn to fly.
Now, though he can zoom all around town,
If he's hungry, he will drop by.

Emile Carstens (13)
Borden Grammar School

The Weatherman

The weatherman, the weatherman,
When he's right, he is a great man.
But one bleak day he wanted perfect weather,
So he could sunbathe with his wife, Heather.
So he waved his hand and made some hail,
But it bounced off the head of his daughter, Gail.
He waved it again and conjured up rain,
But he got as wet as a sunken plane.
He saluted again and thought of thunder,
But it scared a man on a cliff so he plundered.
Then he thought of sun and it appeared,
And he was as warm as an old man's beard.

Jordan Arthurs (13)
Borden Grammar School

Cricket

In the open field,
The sun up high,
A man hits a ball,
It goes to the sky.

He uses a bat,
It's made out of wood,
This game is cricket
And it's easily understood.

A man bowls a ball,
It speeds to the batsman very fast,
He hits the ball so very hard,
People said that ball was bigger in the past.

Higher and higher that ball rose,
Past an aeroplane from Montserrat,
Then it dropped
And then, 'Howzat!'

Mitchell Payne (13)
Borden Grammar School

My Letter Poem For WWI

In the recent form of events,
I hope you see the sense,
For I have joined the army,
Before you say, I'm not barmy!
See I will die a man,
Join me if you can,
Together we will stand side by side with Britain
While everyone reads this letter I have written.
Some will leave their hearts, bodies and souls,
Fighting for the pride of Britain, in enormous man-made holes,
For here my letter concludes,
Come help us fight the feuds.

Mark Cryer (13)
Borden Grammar School

The White Ripples

There I am, standing on a plain white floor,
Looking around me, nothing but white,
Endless miles of white,
Silent.
Suddenly I feel pulses,
Again and again.
I look around to see tiny white ripples
In the distance, looking like the sea
On a peaceful day,
Until I notice the ripples get bigger,
Or maybe closer?
I start to run in the other direction
But then freeze.
Ripples that side as well,
Ripples all around me,
I am trapped.
As I stand there, the ripples become waves,
The waves become tsunamis.
Closer and closer they come,
Crash!
They bounce back and slowly sink into the ground,
Plain, silent, white.

Lewis Wilde (13)
Borden Grammar School

Moment

The stars shine so brightly in the sky,
The moon shines so sweetly,
A cold, crisp moment of calm,
A glimpse of peace away from life . . .
Everything sleeps,
A puddle of dawn,
As a single drop of light begins
To flood my little world.

Samuel Johnston (14)
Borden Grammar School

Air

When I think of the air,
I think of freedom and life, plants and flowers,
Trees, birds and bees and survival.

The precious air we love to share
Brings joy, health and happiness.

Then come the cars, the factories,
The trains and the plane,
And look what they've done to our beautiful air!

The ice is melting, the seas are warming,
The storms are raging and the Earth is shaking.
We saw this coming and just did nothing.
What have we done?
We've destroyed our air we loved to share!

Is it too late?

Damian Kelly (15)
Borden Grammar School

The Ferrari

The stunning figure approached;
The silky body, gleaming and shimmering.
The polished wheels were spinning
As if there was no end.

The elegant machine grew closer,
The bloodshot-red colour
Was bursting out at me,
The roar of the mighty engine - devastating!

It had such class, and the polished,
Fulgent smile of the paintwork
Was dazzling my delicate eyes,
Which were hooked on the truly marvelous vehicle.

Samuel Collins (14)
Borden Grammar School

The Towers

On a tour bus in New York
There was a man
With a camcorder,
With his wife
And children,
On holiday.
Under the Towers he was
With his camcorder,
With his wife
And children
On holiday.
Enjoying his holiday
With his camcorder,
With his wife
And children
On holiday.
He saw them coming
With his camcorder,
With his wife
And children
On holiday.
Saw them crash
With his camcorder,
With his wife
And children
On holiday.
There is a man in a cemetery
With his camcorder,
Without his wife
And children,
All alone.

Jamie Martin (13)
Borden Grammar School

The Storm!

The ferocious storm
Is far from the norm

Headed for the Americas
To stop the summer scorches

The alarm is raised
And the sun is hazed

The wind, it blows
Some boats it throws

The trees go down
Throughout the town

Here come the waves
As the storm slaves

The flood comes in
Away floats a bin

The sound level's dropping
The last tree is flopping

The wind is now easing
Boy that *is* pleasing

The water just sits there
Without any care

Bearing disease
That's not gonna please . . .

Charlie Bowling (13)
Borden Grammar School

Glorious War?

War is not good nor pleasant. War is never short, only long,
In which loads of innocent men die in a place they don't belong.
Most soldiers die a horrible, gruesome death,
And the ones that live on often turn out deaf
War sends men crazy, they become shell-shocked,
They become so scared that in their minds everyone else
                                            gets blocked.

Can you imagine watching your best friend die?
Trust me, you don't want to,
So don't enlist in the army just to try.

You may think you will come back a hero,
You probably will, in a coffin carried by friends and co.
But the saddest thing of all
Isn't if the war is big or small,
It's the people who start the war. They don't fight!
They plot the attacks from miles away and then just hide!

You also have to feel for the soldiers' friends and family
Who every night get on their knees and hope their little boy is
                                            all right.
Can you imagine being told your son is almost certain to die?
You would curl up in a ball and cry and cry!

So don't talk about war as if it is good,
Put yourself in a soldier's shoes and you might just understand
That no war is great or glamorous!

So what is the point?

Andrew Taylor (13)
Borden Grammar School

The Lone Star

Travelling alone within the company of the stars in the sky
The lone traveller walks down the dusty track.
Awake by night he is on his way, does he know where?
Of course not, no.
By day he sleeps in bush, tree or cabin,
Resting all day so he's ready for the night ahead.
Does he know when he will arrive?
Of course not, no.
He knows not when his journey will end,
In desert, track, country, city or sea.
He is like a star in the day, alone and desperate to be free.
Free from what? Does he know?
Of course not, no.
One night when walking on his own,
Heard a sound did our lone star.
Looking back he sees the thing that fills him with dread,
The dangerous foes of those on the road.
Marauders hunting, does he know why?
Of course not, no.
The traveller falls, a bullet in his back,
Red blood in the moonlight.
Looks up at the sky, sees the stars and he is rising up.
The lone star to join them all.
His journey done, he sighs, does he know why?
Of course not, no.

Mitchell Prentice (13)
Borden Grammar School

The Crowd

I heard the crowd that was there,
I saw a crowd of people through the misty air.
I was on my way to a stadium,
I saw the red flare made from lithium.
I parked outside Camp Nou,
I got out and needed the loo.

I went in and found my seat,
Everyone was singing along to the beat.
Everyone went silent for the National Anthem,
The players had hands on hearts and fans sang with them.
The whistle went and everyone screamed,
This was the best game of the year, it seemed.

The ball was played,
The shot was beautifully aimed.
The shot went in and there was a cheer.
People said, 'Cheers', and drank some beer.
My dad said, 'This is good.'
And we were all in a good mood.

Daniel Gebbie (14)
Borden Grammar School

The Reptile

He sleeps all day,
He's awake all night,
He's awake in the dark,
But asleep in the light.

He sleeps when there's no food,
He's awake when he's fed,
You might find him quite rude,
But better rude than dead.

This is my lizard's life,
He might sound boring,
He might sound dumb,
But to me he sounds pretty fun.

Jack Matthews (13)
Borden Grammar School

A Beaker Poem

From the day it was invented,
It was always argumentative.
No one ever found a name
But found it a big pain.
To have a confusing piece of junk
Cluttering up your room.
No one ever found a use,
They just gave it abuse.
If you have no occupation,
Why not try finding a use
For this confusing piece of junk
That no one ever found a name for
Until Einstein came along and said,
'What should I call you?'
And so to this day it remains
A confusing piece of junk.

Conrad Fry (13)
Borden Grammar School

The Field Of Cheese

I look across a field of cheese
As I feel a gentle breeze.
It looks like the cheese will never end,
But in the distance I see my friend.
I see him with the Queen of Cheese,
As I call, 'Oh, help me please.'
The Queen of Cheese flies over to me,
She looks so graceful, like a bee.
She tells me that the cheese will disappear,
Then so will my right ear.
So the cheese disappears and I fall from the sky,
I think, *oh my God, I'm going to die.*
I fall on my head
And wake up, I'm in bed!

Jake Marshall (13)
Borden Grammar School

High Flying

My grip has been loosened,
I can feel myself getting higher!
I can feel the wind gushing around me
As if I am being smothered.

The sky is a baby blue, only to be seen by
The birds, not appreciated by anyone.
The people below take no notice of me up above,
Swooping and floating higher and higher.

They are all but a speck of dust to me,
I have not a care in the world.
The buildings look jagged and out of place,
As if nature never intended for them to be there.

The world seems insignificant now,
I have found where I need to be, a place of happiness.
Peaceful and quiet, not a care in the world.
The floor below me seems unreachable and looks so small.

The boy who let me go has probably forgotten me now,
Just a distant memory in his immature brain.
I wonder how much longer I will go
Until I reach a drastic end?

It is just nice to think though,
That I am all alone, calm and peaceful.
Not a trouble in the world
And lost in a sea of clouds.

Beau August (14)
Borden Grammar School

We Are The Soldiers

We are the soldiers that lay in trenches day and night.
We are the soldiers who have lost the desire and will to fight.

We are the soldiers who risk our lives for you.
We are the soldiers that have to attain our due.

We are the soldiers that have to put up with evil stagnant smells.
We are the soldiers that launch and dodge shells.

We are the soldiers that peer over the verge with our guns.
We are the soldiers who gasp for breath in our gas-filled lungs.

We are the soldiers who cannot complain.
We are the soldiers that are suffering pain.

We are the soldiers that are deprived of our friends.
We are the soldiers who have reached our heroic ends.

Jackson Shaddick (14)
Borden Grammar School

Out In Space

'In space, no one can hear you scream!'
That's what the man said to his friend.
As the shuttle climbed, the engines started to strain,
Then it burst through the atmosphere and then, silence.

The shuttle started to turn towards the sun.
The man realised the mission had begun.
All of a sudden there was a bang,
The shuttle started to roll over.

The man realised he was going to die,
He was going to explode like a squashed fly.
The sun shone through the windows
And the temperature started to climb.
The shuttle went bang and the mission was over.

Michael Barton (15)
Borden Grammar School

Who Is To Blame?

Angels fill Heaven,
Demons fill Hell,
Humans in the middle
Destroying their once green land.
The world is changing,
But who is to blame?

Could it be the inventors
For making cars and bombs?
Could it be the government,
For ruling everyone?
But I say no,
I know the truth.

Everyone in the world's to blame.
We pollute, we litter,
We do it every day.
People are to blame.
Is it too late to stop,
Stop the end of the world?

Tommy Chapman (13)
Borden Grammar School

In Twenty Years Time . . .

In twenty years time,
Will the weather still be fine?

Will it be hot,
Will it be cold,
Will we have to be skinny,
Will we have to be bold?

In twenty years time,
What will I be like?

Will I be smart,
Will I be a lazy fart,
Will I be well-dressed,
Will I be a total mess?

In twenty years time,
Who will I be?

I know who I'll be,
Whatever the weather,
Whatever I'm like,
I will still be me!

Daniel Glazier (14)
Borden Grammar School

Spain

Spain, it's as if it's on the edge of the world,
Beauty at its finest!

Clear blue waters,
As if someone's laid a pearl-blue sheet.

The sun seems to leap at you,
It's a different kind of heat.

The burning air is so intense,
As if we are under a magnifying glass.

Sleeping until afternoon
(It's the only place you'll get away with it)

The long laze for the rest
And the hyped-up nights

You've never seen anything like it!

Drunk people staggering around,
Parents keeping little ones away from them

The whole family in the pub
Enjoying life while it lasts

Everyone exhausted,
Time to go home!

Michael Wood (14)
Borden Grammar School

My Nan

She is sitting all alone,
Should I sit with her?
She is sitting in silence,
Should I talk to her?
She is so very hungry,
Should I give her some food?
She is cold,
Should I give her a blanket?
She needs to be loved,
Should I tell her I love her?
She is my nan,
My lonely, silent, hungry, cold, unloved nan.
But she isn't really any of those things.
She has Alzheimer's disease and she doesn't realise.
We keep her company, we talk to her,
We give her food and warmth,
And we love her too,
But she doesn't know,
She just doesn't know!

Michael Camber (13)
Borden Grammar School

Child Soldier

All alone sits a boy in a field of death,
His father's in prison, his mother is dead.
When he was young, he was happy,
He played with his mum,
Then soldiers came, shot her
And put an end to his fun.
They took him and trained him,
Taught him to kill,
To become a murderer, a killer,
Like a plague, if you will.
They gave him a gun,
An AK47,
And he believed when he died
He would not go to Heaven.
He fought in a war,
While all his friends died,
They collapsed beside him,
No life in their eyes.
Now he sits alone in a field of death
And of the bodies around him,
None draw breath.

Adam Pilfold Bagwell (13)
Borden Grammar School

The Big Push

The sun emerges upon the hill,
Awakening the men who live to kill.

With tired eyes, which seem so dim,
They left their dugouts without a whim.

Their bayonets they take in hand,
Staring out at no-man's-land.

Saddened hearts filled with fear,
Waiting now, death is near.

Frightened by the horrors ahead,
Soon their friends will be all dead.

All in silence, as though in prayer,
Their haunted thoughts, they do not share.

The end has come as whistles blow.
Marching now, it's time to go.

Determined, they climb up over the top,
Screams of pain as men get shot.

A solemn place, so many killed,
Now a peaceful poppy field.

Kylie Newport (17)
Chatham Grammar School for Girls

Winter's Thaw

I shake through the heavy winter snow,
Inside there's a hot, juicy roast.
I sleep and dream of diamond-white ice,
Crystallizing as the wind blows.
Outside a puppy cries in the frozen wind,
His sadness invades my dream.

I wake up to a cup of hot chocolate with thick cream on top.
My hair is a mess.
I am snug in my pyjamas, curled up on the sofa.
A nagging concern for that poor lost dog at the back of my mind.

A worrying damp smell invades the house.
Now I get my boots on,
Drag on my coat and gloves and open the door.
Bam, guess what?
The snow has gone, the snowman is nowhere to be seen.
Spring is here.
A droopy-eyed puppy has captured my heart.

Looch Trevor (12)
East Court School for Dyslexia

Chocolate Cake

I ate the cake,
I knew I shouldn't have,
But it was scrummy, it was yummy.

I was the witness,
I saw him, he knew he shouldn't.
I thought he wouldn't,
But he did.

I was the cake.
I saw the boy with his greedy claw
And his nasty paw.

Petrok Lawrence (11)
East Court School for Dyslexia

The Food Chain

I'm a sleek, predatory cat,
As black as a shiny raven's feather.
I'm as brave and as fierce as a knight at war,
As bloody as Sweeny Todd.
I'm sneaky, I'm sly and I'm proud of it.

I'm a silvery, shiny, timid mouse.
I slip through holes when I'm running away.
I steal some food, I do not share,
We are all hungry here.

I'm a cruel, evil spider.
My webs entice my prey and trap them to their death.
I can be a friendly little house spider,
But when I see a fly, *splat,* he's dead!

Jack Walker (12)
East Court School for Dyslexia

Mixed Emotions

Pleasure is an ice cream slowly melting in your hand.
Happiness is sitting watching the sunset on a beach.
Delight is the first day of summer.
Shock is when you can't believe that something could be so good.

Betrayal is when someone you trusted lets you down.
Sadness is when someone important upsets you.
Disappointment is when something you wanted to happen doesn't
Panic is when your worries come true.
Disbelief is when you can't believe something so bad could happen.
Misery is when you are really unhappy.

Emotionally exhausted is when you are so tired of all your emotions.

Luke Lennard (11)
East Court School for Dyslexia

Great, The New Menu

My career is on the line,
I must prepare a special meal,
A meal for the Lord Mayor of London.
I am very nervous, scared that I will lose my job.
I have not found a recipe book to help me,
Nothing is appropriate for this situation.
I am frustrated, cross and irritable.
Inspiration strikes.

Meat drizzled with rosé wine and cheesy baked potatoes,
The crisp, golden-brown sausages cook fast,
Honey-roasted ham with baby boiled potatoes
Smothered in rich blue cheese.
Thousands of deep yellow egg yolks frying,
Buttery zucchini pie full of different taste.
Cooling stew of game and vegetables,
Or sweet peach bun for dessert.
Creamy white wine soup with a spicy kick,
Oysters and beans boiling in hot water, what a delicacy.

It is done, thank goodness.
He will be hired soon.
I'd better get this cooking.
God, I hope he likes this, I worked my hardest.
Please say he will like it, or I will need a new job.

Richard Atkins (12)
East Court School for Dyslexia

Chemicals In Our Food

I'm not a baby, I can eat what I want.
The farmers are upset, they're not paid enough,
So one made a drug that makes the crops really big.
When people saw them they were amazed.
It's not right making them that big.

Enormous vegetables make my blood go cold.
Mushrooms the size of my mother,
Zucchini the girl next door can't carry,
Haricot vert too numerous to microwave,
They are so repulsive I can never eat, only scream.

Frozen peas the size of soup tins,
The candy is running out.
Flavours are not so nice with the taste of veg in your mouth,
Sweets are not sweet,
Fries are not fries
And chocolate tastes of fat.

Then people realise the truth,
It makes you grow a beard.
All the girls are angry, the boys don't care.
It is funny how it turned out.
A week later, I'm eating sweets.

James Hawkins (13)
East Court School for Dyslexia

War

War is grotty, war is sad.
War is lucky - when you're in a trench.
In war you shout and men go down next to you.
Bombs and grenades are thrown at you.
You fall and see the mass of people dead around you.
The machine gun deafens you when you are crawling through
                                    the muddy ground,
Then you hear a piercing whistle above the guns.
It means go back to your trench.
You fall in,
Crushed by bodies that fall on you.
The stench of rotten flesh is horrible,
Scattered around like dog meat.
Then go to sleep, hoping there isn't a raid.
No bombs and shells thrown during the night.
You fall asleep.
There's heavy gunfire, shots at the Germans,
There is a raid.
The only thing keeping you sane is wanting to see your wife,
But every day that dream vanishes,
Because you are on the frontline.

Giles Sparkes (12)
East Court School for Dyslexia

The Beach

It's sunrise, the sea caresses the sand.
It's sunrise, the birds sing melodies to their babies.
It's sunrise, you can hear the sound of scuttling crabs.
It's sunrise, the sand is wet and crunchy after last night's rain.
When I see this I feel a calm and peaceful ecstasy.

It's afternoon, the children are running and shouting.
It's afternoon, the toddlers are in rubber rings on the waves.
It's afternoon, you can smell the barbecues made by anxious dads.
It's afternoon the mums are trying to sunbathe in vain.
When I see this I feel a happy and excited joy.

It's sunset, the peaceful feeling of quiet.
It's sunset, the seagulls perching on forgotten sandcastles.
It's sunset, the mother birds soar back to put their chicks under
their wings.
It's sunset, the sea gives a goodnight kiss to the sand.
When I see this I feel a pleased and serene tranquillity.

Bethany Parrott (11)
East Court School for Dyslexia

Love

Cooking is my prime passion.
I love cooking, even when I'm down it lifts me up
And turns me around.
The smell of my mum's cooking makes my mouth water.
Chocolate cake and crispy bacon, hot toast with golden butter,
Lovely roast potatoes, nestling round a steaming joint.
This is the bond I have with my mum.
She fed me when I was small,
She feeds me now.
She loves me and I love her.
When she is old, it will be my turn to cook for her,
To show her how much I love her.
And I really, really love her.

Edmund Robinson (12)
East Court School for Dyslexia

The Cloud Wolf

'Twas on a chilly winter's eve,
Clouds of mist whenever I breathe.
There I stood in silent wonder,
Hearing the distant rumble of thunder.

A majestic creature stood before me,
Swirling tendrils of electricity.
Advanced swiftly, did the beast,
From the direction of the east.

Huge black clouds gathered in the sky,
Lightning bright enough to blind the eye.

The great black cloud which was the beast,
Opened its mouth, for on discomfort it does feast.
Torrents of rain came lashing down,
Puddles of panic all around.

Women and children flee to stay alive,
Like many bees from a hive.
Screaming and wailing,
Wading and hopeless sailing.

Huge black clouds gathered in the sky,
Lightning bright enough to blind the eye.

I stood there watching to the end,
Watched the angels God did send.
Not one person was left alive,
There were no more bees left in the hive.
'Twas no big surprise,
The bloodied flood water did hastily rise.

A land of terror and destruction before me,
However, the cloud wolf I did see,
Feasting on the devastation.

Kayleigh Vidler (12)
Folkestone School for Girls

To The Beast

A monstrous beast so elegant,
Duelling in perfect rhythm with the sky.
No limitation to its all the time performance.
But held by the harness of metallic reality,
And yet, with all its grace, the walk
Into the midst of human excitement is
Still one only the high will take.
A break, so everyone has stopped.

Every emotion is still heard
But there is still an overwhelming
Shudder as the beast flies past us.
Heads look up, we shall tame it soon.
The screech of wheels on metal,
And a breeze whips across our faces
And we continue our voyage through
Unnecessary boundaries.

The mass diverged. 'Do we want the front?'
'No!' So the endless walk continues
and daring to leave the flock,
whilst the others continue forward.
Conversation is at peak and
I feel . . . Fear? Excitement? Unsure.
A rush sensation, two and two,
We have already arranged.
And now it is our turn to tame the
Beast that calls upon us.

Miriam Tresh (16)
Folkestone School for Girls

Rugby Is Life

There's a rush of excitement as you wander through the crowds
Looking for your seat.
You are a spectator of everything around you.
You hear and feel every kick, every touch of the ball.
You hear the contracting of every muscle,
The focusing of every eye.
You have your position in the crowd,
People are screaming louder and louder,
Encouragement and shouts fill your ears
Until you don't know who's shouting what!
Confusion and fear takes over.
The conversion flies over the goal for one final glorious high.
Then the final whistle blows.
It's over as fast as it had begun.
There are drinks, celebrators and mourners
Murmuring into their pints, 'Good game',
But it makes no difference, they can't change the outcome.

Laura Logan (16)
Folkestone School for Girls

The Snowflake

Glistening, floating from up high,
Silver tones caught against the
Dark of night. Gliding gracefully,
Its splendour shown in the wisp

Of street lamps. Towards its bed
Of white it travels easily,
Weaving through the harsh winter,
So delicate and intricate.

Glistening, floating from up high.
I catch it. It glides no more.

Vicki White (16)
Folkestone School for Girls

Hazel Brown Horses

Hazel brown horses with hazel brown eyes
Tossing their manes to get rid of the flies.
Hazel brown horses with hazel brown eyes,
Watching the butterfly fluttering by.

Crystal white horses with crystal white eyes,
Closely watching the dragonflies.
Crystal white horses with crystal white eyes,
Looking up to the light blue sky.

Glossy black horses with glossy black eyes,
Keeping a close eye on the passers-by.
Glossy black horses with glossy black eyes,
Staring directly at the apples nearby.

Sunshine gold horses with sunshine gold eyes,
Trotting around in hot July.
Sunshine gold horses with sunshine gold eyes,
Listening to the strong breeze cry.

Joelle Wade (11)
Folkestone School for Girls

Stars

Shining brightly through the night
As the darkness climbs in,
The moon appears from behind dark clouds
And the magic of the night is here.

The stars cast their spell as they glisten
And the moon shines down like a torch.
The sunset is completely gone now
And the magic of the night is here.

In the soundless sleep of the day,
The sun will be waking soon,
So we all need to cherish the moments
When the magic of the night is here.

Sarah Beech (11)
Folkestone School for Girls

The Day After Christmas

Baubles glint in the bitter-cold morning light,
The children are still in bed this day.
Today there are no joyful shouts,
No, the house is silent and still.

The tree still stands, stripped of brightly-coloured parcels,
The adults lay asleep dreaming, remembering.
Today there are no noisy carols being sung,
No, the house is silent and still.

Tinsel glitters as the golden sunlight peeps in the curtains,
The dog is curled cosily in its basket.
Today there are no excited yelps,
No, the house is silent and still.

In her crib the baby stirs,
No need to wake, little one.
Your first is over,
For today is the day after Christmas.

Jennifer Towell (15)
Folkestone School for Girls

Untitled

As I close my eyes, I see a new world,
I tumble on green, rich grass.
As I open my eyes, I see the bright sky
With fluffy clouds floating by.
I realise this is real, no fake fantasy.
I realise this is no lie, that this is reality.
The sweet, glorious melody of the elegant nightingale,
It's love is sweet when it flies gracefully,
Even though it flew away, it'll always stay in my memory.
The day is nearly passing by,
It'll be happening for eternity.
The sunset goes by, then the night appears in the dark sky.
The shooting star springs with force as I make a wish,
This has been a journey that I will keep, but I will also miss!

Brinsha Rai (11)
Folkestone School for Girls

A Day In The Life Of My Cat, Sammy

When I get up in the morning and have a wee,
I go and wash my paws and have breakfast.
Then I go to my sister's. We chased a fly,
I'm loving eating the tasty treat.
It doesn't put me off my lunch
Like *someone* I know!
I have a nap and dream of all sorts,
I have loads and loads and loads of these.
Then she comes in from school and wakes me up.
I'm totally disgusted, but happy.
I take my dinner off her plate,
Complete an act of vandalism on the sofa,
Fight with my sisters, Sox and Sooty,
Eat my owner's hair . . . then I sleep, *at last!*

Natasha Sleeman (12)
Folkestone School for Girls

Springtime Awakening

The ice cracks, winter thaws,
Numb trees shake off their frosty coats.
The hedgerow shivers under the pale sky
And birds stretch their wings and sing.
The hedgehog and badger awake from sleep
To find autumn reds now springtime yellow.
Daffodils tentatively push up through the earth
And spread their sunny gold message to all.
Ewes find springtime joy in lambs,
Stumbling and uncertain in the lush green field.
Recovering flowers are rescued by butterflies
Who ease them with their colourful wings.
The heavens are open with the awakening of nature
And the birds, trees and animals begin to sing.

Abbie Sims (16)
Folkestone School for Girls

The Swimming Pool

One day I went to the swimming pool,
It was really, really cool.
Slowly I stepped in,
Frequently bashing my chin.
Suddenly there was a splash,
Loudly, it was my dad diving with a great crash.
Eventually I got out,
Easily climbing up the ladder
With a great shout,
Effectively jumping off the board,
While in the air praising the Lord.
For this incredible place, recently built,
Is the brightest place to be.
The pool is calm and still
While people are having a meal.
There is a canteen over there
With quite a lot of chairs.
Amazingly the changing rooms
Are a bunch of rooms.
The jacuzzi is a bubbly place,
Everybody has a smile on their face.

Shannon Petrie (11)
Folkestone School for Girls

The Mountain Spring

The ground begins to tremble on a lonely mountainside.
Fighting through the rocks and stones searching for the light,
A little spring bursts forth, it can no longer hide.
Joyfully jumping to be free, it glistens clear and bright.

Skipping over every pebble, the stream begins to grow,
Rushing over jagged stones with its speed increasing,
No rock too big to challenge the ice-cold crystal flow,
And on and on it runs with energy never ceasing.

Rachel Thomas (16)
Folkestone School for Girls

Beautifully Broken

Oh she's been stupid, but she's been beautiful
And she doesn't deserve how they treat her.
The last time she smiled
Was with those of another culture, another life!

How could someone be so different
To these the same as her?
Yet so similar,
To those so unlike her?

She hides behind that Indonesian mask
And reveals blind faith, of how she plans
To escape and get out of the places
Where she never doubted she didn't belong.

Idaho calls and she takes a breath,
The sand silences
As she touches it with her toes.
The kestrels fly above, knowing themselves.

But before she knows it, she returns
To those who don't understand the real her.
The religion is out of her body as she reflects
And she realises she's dead again.

Lauran Jarvis (13)
Folkestone School for Girls

Snake!

I am a smooth snake, a long snake, searching on my own.
I am a poisonous snake, an angry snake, always having to moan.
I am a scaly snake, a quiet snake, waiting for my food.
I am an aggressive snake, a nasty snake, trying to be a dude.
I am a hungry snake, a funny snake, going out into the night.
I am a colourful snake, a plain snake, ready for a fight.
I am a small snake, a skinny snake, finding life hard.

Alexis Noonan (11)
Folkestone School for Girls

My Empty Canvas

Words swirl within my mind,
I sit and wait.
What word will leap at me next?
I wait to find.

Time running out; pen bled dry,
Thoughts thundering in my mind.
Pen to paper; will not reach.
I stare at my empty canvas.

Nothing more, nothing less,
Inspiration will not take me
To use my creativity
And plaster this empty canvas once again.

I sit prepared, just like you,
Waiting for a miracle,
Waiting for a miracle,
Yet it escapes once again.

Awaiting my captivating creativity,
The blanket of emptiness
Screams out to me
Like a dreaded nightmare.

My mind is locked away.
Words have died.
No more to say.
I sit and wait.

Bubbling, bursting in my mind,
Thoughts swirl till I feel blind.
Pen finally reaches paper,
Yet my canvas remains empty . . .

Stephanie Mackenzie (16)
Folkestone School for Girls

9/11

For every brick there was a life,
For every life there was a loss
And for every loss there was pain.

They used to stand tall and proud,
Like they were the centre of attention
And on this day they were
As the news sent our world crashing down.

For every brick there was a life,
For every life there was a loss
And for every loss there was pain.

The aftermath was a shocking sight,
Something we will never forget in a hurry,
And five years on we still mourn,
As names and faces still lie missing on paper.

For every brick there was a life,
For every life there was a loss
And for every loss there was pain.

Danielle Thorpe-Gray (16)
Folkestone School for Girls

I Am A Snake

I hiss and I slide,
I have nothing to hide.
Why do they scream and run?
I am only young.
All alone in a big glass box,
Torn away from family and friends.
I am scared,
I am sad,
I'm not big,
I'm not bad,
I'm just a smooth, sweet, kind, loveable snake.

Aimee Irving (12)
Folkestone School for Girls

Farewell

My pen is floating above paper.
Hesitating, longing to leak
All over the page. But how can
I write what my mind
Thinks of so powerfully?
As to leave him alone in the darkness.
Tears of despair falling
Down his cheek.
The pen leaves marks all over
Our surroundings desperate
To be connected as one with paper.
And then, like a flash of light
I am struck with a will,
A will so strong that my companion
Takes the burden from my shoulders.
My pen is floating above paper,
Satisfied.

Laura Winstanley (16)
Folkestone School for Girls

Anna Maria Island!

Around Anna Maria Island you can see
Hundreds of squirrels running nervously
Around the palm trees.

And the slimy stingrays aren't hard to miss
When swimming silently with them on a daily basis,
You get used to them frequently gliding past you.

The dolphins glide effortlessly above the calm waves,
Early in the morning, the dolphins swim
Smoothly along the sea.

Pelicans are one of my favourites of all,
Especially when they seem to casually fly above you
And land awkwardly two feet away,
Trying to sneakily steal the fisherman's catch.

Ellie Carter-Leay (11)
Folkestone School for Girls

A Thousand Words

A pen in my hand
To explore my passion,
But where do I start?
I'm just another girl
Ready to share her heart.

I could write a thousand words
About my intense love for him,
I could write a thousand words
Of how my day's been going.

I could write a thousand words
Of the things I'd like to see.
I could write a thousands words
Of who I dream to be.

But on writing these thousand words
I wouldn't know where to begin.
Poetry is emotional,
Illustrated from within.

Victoria Castle (15)
Folkestone School for Girls

Butterfly

The wind was still so I held my breath,
The air was hot and sticky to feel,
The sun was glowing and shining high,
The sky was empty, as clear as clear.
I stopped to watch,
I dare not move or mutter a sound,
All I could do was quietly watch
A beautiful butterfly sat gently in front of me,
With its rainbow of golden colour shimmering in the ray of sun,
And its dusty wings flittering faster than the eye could see,
Its hairy caterpillar body still there to see,
It's been through a long and wonderful journey.
How wonderful it sat there, quietly, just for me.

Jessica Maynard (11)
Folkestone School for Girls

The School Rush

Getting up for school is always a rush,
From underneath my bed I grab my brush,
Daily and lazily I puff up my quilt,
Sleepily but quickly I chuck on my kilt.

Safely I jump down the carpeted stairs,
Laying the table and pulling out chairs.
On my plate lays bacon and eggs,
Fidget, the dog, underneath my legs.

Rushing to the bathroom I get to the sink,
Grabbing my toothbrush that happens to be pink.
Away in the cupboard the toothpaste does sit,
There down the plughole goes my salivary spit.

Suddenly I realise the time on the clock,
I slip my shoe over the top of my sock.
Speedily I rush and slam the door,
Nervously crossing the road once more.

Madeleine Ubee (11)
Folkestone School for Girls

My Poem

I walked to the door briskly,
I slowly pulled it open,
I stepped out cautiously in case anyone was watching,
I shut the door in complete silence,
I started to run,
Not just any old run, a run that was quick,
Nerve-wracking and a little bit strained,
As if there was something bothering me,
But then as I got into the run I started to relax,
I sighed heavily, making my body slouch forwards,
I was finally alone,
Somewhere where I could think and concentrate on myself,
Somewhere other than home.

Hannah Dinnage (11)
Folkestone School for Girls

The Haunted House

It was on a winter's night in mid-December,
I'll tell you the story of how much I can remember.
I was walking on a road and what did I see?
A pathway leading to houses, not one but three.
I closed my eyes and went ip-dip-doo,
Guess where it landed? Path number two.
I carried on walking, on and on I went,
To a weird abandoned house all crooked and bent.
I knocked on the door, no answer came,
I soon gave up and thought the plan was lame.
As I turned my back, I heard a sound,
Frantically enough I spun right round.
There was nothing there as I looked left and right,
I had my fists out, preparing to fight.
The door was open so I walked in,
And on the wall in blood read *You've committed a sin.*
The door slammed shut, I cried and knelt,
My eyes were all puffy, I thought I was going to be killed.
I heard a voice, more like a moan,
I stopped sobbing and gave a groan.
I stood up and thought crying was dumb,
But as I strolled around, I felt really numb.
I then saw this person and had to scream and shout,
But with a swing of his bat, I got knocked out.
That was how the story went, how I suffered the pain,
But when I opened my eyes, I wasn't standing in the rain.
That's what happened on a winter's night in mid-December,
I've now told the story, as much as I can remember.

Sanjidah Islam (11)
Folkestone School for Girls

Your Nightmares . . .

It was the dead of the night,
I could see the midnight moon
Shining through the thick pine trees.
I saw the flapping wings of the bats,
Their sharp claws hanging onto the branch of the tree,
Ready to catch me . . .
I could hear the screech of an owl
From a nearby tree,
Maybe hooting a warning signal.
I could suddenly feel something.
Something crawling on my back.
So often, I could smell an awful pong
From the foul, dead, eaten rats.
But now as I ambled through the overgrown forest,
Towards the light,
There was no sight of vicious flapping bats,
There was no sound from the hooting owls,
There was no feeling of the creature crawling up my back,
There was no awful pong of dead, eaten rats.
I didn't get it. What was happening?

Ruby McCaffrey (11)
Folkestone School for Girls

An Autumn Day

Autumn leaves slowly falling from their branches,
Conkers cracking among the daily passers,
The wind picks up and is blowing very briskly,
Through people's hair it flows very swiftly.

Children kicking and playing with the brown crispy leaves,
Branches swaying in the almighty strong breeze,
Toddlers playing in the park,
Flying their kites until it is dark.

The clouds move in and the burst of rain
Hits against the glass windowpane,
Soggy washing dragging on the line,
Now it is the children's bedtime.

Awake in the morning, rise and shine,
Still it is raining, no sunshine,
Wellington boots splashing on the ground,
Listening to the lovely splashy sound.

Raincoats, umbrellas, dripping slowly in the porchway,
What a lovely time we had today.
The little sleepyheads getting ready for bed.
Shh . . .

Kiera Ward (11)
Folkestone School for Girls

Released From Reality

Reality is such a bore,
Monotonous days, same old nights,
Living becomes a chore,
With the same, repeated sights.
Over and over and over,
And we sigh, as we know
Tomorrow shall be today,
And we sigh, as we go,
About doing what we did yesterday.
I long for change, I long for spice,
For colours to seep in.
I want out of this sickeningly nice
Reality we are trapped within.
Your happiness, my anger, our pain,
I want us to feel once more,
I can't follow the crowd, can't be the same,
I have to be free, like I know I was before.
And when the walls of this cage
Break down around me,
I will take a clean page
And write a new story.
And then there will be
No pattern to follow, no path to tread,
My journey won't be based on reality,
Rather the stories born inside my head.

Ruth Wilkie (14)
Folkestone School for Girls

The Life Of A Troubled Girl

She lies in her bed all cosy and warm,
Whimpering and shaking over the long, loud storm.
Gradually getting up and running for her teddy,
Making sure she is nice and steady.
A girl, five years old, scared to run to her mum in case she might
                                                    get a beating,
She heard her voice getting closer as she was speaking.
Her mum opened the door, shouting and blazing,
The girl sat in the corner crying like crazy.
Her mum raised her hand and slapped it down on the girl.
'I knew it, you are a thief, you stole my pearls,' the mum beamed.
The girl sat there in the corner and said nothing, too scared to get
                                                    another beating.

The next day she woke up and called Childline,
She listened to someone speaking.
They came and put her mum in jail
And put the girl in a foster home without fail.

Jessica Park (12)
Fort Pitt Grammar School for Girls

Under The Ocean

The ocean is a wonderful, beautiful place!
The fish are always having a relay race.
The seaweed flows among the sand,
While the mermaids dance, hand in hand.
The sharks try to catch their prey,
They always succeed, every single day.
The dazzling pearls are the fairest of them all,
Partly because they're shaped like a tiny little ball.
All the sea creatures have a unique face,
The ocean is a wonderful, beautiful place!

Reanna Walters (11)
Fort Pitt Grammar School for Girls

In My World

In my world I'd like to see
Chocolate trees and money bees.
To climb a mountain up and down,
To never see anyone wear a frown.
To have a little brother that's not a pain,
Miracles happen, sounds insane.
Travel through time and into space,
And it would be great not to have to pack my case.
Have a world full of peace and grace,
But I can't live without a few debates,
Help out the poor and visit the rich.

If I could understand boys and their strange little world,
Then maybe I could find a perfect match
For everyone and somebody for me.
To travel round the world, over the land and the seas.
So that's what I would like.
What would you like?

Elena Smitherman (11)
Fort Pitt Grammar School for Girls

Christmas is . . .

Christmas is Celebrated every year by everyone.
Christmas is Hilarious, a time for smiling and fun.
Christmas is Romantic, full of love and joy.
Christmas is Infectious, be ready to annoy.
Christmas is Super duper, gigantic and big.
Christmas is Temptation, my grandad loves a fig.
Christmas is Mouthwatering, warm and full of cheer.
Christmas is Annual, it comes every year.
Christmas is Santa, pressies all round!

Hannah Smith (11)
Fort Pitt Grammar School for Girls

Extending Love And Friendship

Friendship is water,
It flows, it splashes,
It stops, it's hard to find.

Friendship is cotton wool,
It's sensitive, it's absorbent,
It's soft, it's warm,
It's gentle, it's helpful.

Love is an onion,
It hurts, it's spicy,
It's layered, it's soft,
It's a rose, it's dry,
It's strong, it hurts.

Love is a roller coaster,
It stops, it turns,
It twists, it's thrilling,
It's fun, it lasts,
It turns, it's over too quickly,
It's either up or down.

Poems are extended,
It's by me, it's interesting,
It's love, it's friendship,
It's a poem.

But . . .
It's extended, that's what counts.

Sammi-Jo Ferigan (11)
Fort Pitt Grammar School for Girls

My Funny Thoughts Poem

Chocolate cherry tree,
Red and green honeybee,
Bright green hair,
Gives me a scare.
Orange and blue rice,
Red-hot ice,
Fat pink pig,
Loves to dig.
You can't have fun
In the freezing cold sun.
Blue and purple kittens,
Wear green and yellow spotty mittens
And a long, slithery snake
Would make me shake.

Emma Gifford (11)
Fort Pitt Grammar School for Girls

Puppy

Beaten and abused,
Shaven and cold,
In a dark place
All alone,
Left on a doorstep,
Scarred for life,
No one to turn to,
All alone,
Taken in by a
Loving someone,
Cared for and loved,
No more alone.

Zoe Bartlett (11)
Fort Pitt Grammar School for Girls

Blue

The calmness of the colour blue,
The sea coming in and out,
The dolphins jumping up and down,
So quiet, I don't dare shout.

The sadness of the colour blue,
Tears running down my face,
All going really fast,
As if it is a race.

The coldness of the colour blue,
Like icicles and snow,
You have to dress up really warm
To make snowballs to throw.

The happiness of the colour blue,
The bright blue sky,
But all you really need to do
Is go ahead and smile!

Jennifer Woolgrove (12)
Fort Pitt Grammar School for Girls

Football

Sitting in the football stalls,
Watching grown men follow the rules,
Waiting for the final call,
Everyone stand up, here comes the ball!

Up till now it's been a draw,
I wonder what will be the score,
Waiting for the final call,
Everyone stand up, here comes the ball!

The whistle is about to blow,
Wait, they've scored another goal,
Waiting for the final call,
Everyone stand up, here comes the ball!

Kimberley McGee (11)
Fort Pitt Grammar School for Girls

The Haunted House!

The horror house hidden with fear,
But we don't want Hallowe'en near,
The witches cackle,
Draculas tackle,
The horror house hidden with fear!

The horror house hidden with fear,
Hopefully it's not near here,
But don't think you're safe,
They don't have faith,
The horror house hidden with fear!

The horror house hidden with fear,
But we don't want Hallowe'en near,
The witches cackle,
Draculas tackle,
The horror house hidden with fear!

Lucy Smith (11)
Fort Pitt Grammar School for Girls

The Ghost Walks The Corridor

Apparently our school is haunted,
Most of the students are really daunted.
Florence walks the history block,
Sometimes we hear, *knock, knock, knock.*
We don't know if it's Florence Nightingale,
But she sounds like a biting whale.
Apparently if you ring the bell,
She chases you and if you tell
Anyone, this is what she will do,
She follows and curses you.

Corrinne Piper (11)
Fort Pitt Grammar School for Girls

Fox Chase

A paradise of wildlife,
Swans on the lake,
Gracefully swimming,
Was a big mistake.
A hungry fox with bloodshot eyes,
Rugged, scratching fur,
And a mind full of lies,
Its teeth as sharp as needles,
Eyes, lifeless as a stone,
Claws bigger than a clenched fist,
And muscles hard as bone.
It stalked up to the water's edge
With a ghostly, deadly grin,
The swans scattered in terror,
The hunt was about to begin.

The swans were mad with fear,
The fox happy as the sun,
Scratching his claws on the ground
And starting to run,
Picking up speed,
Gaining ground,
Closer and closer
With every bound.
Then it was all over,
One false move from the fox.
The fox as still as he had ever been,
Impaled upon the rocks.

Ayesha Chouglay (11)
Fort Pitt Grammar School for Girls

I'm Just Being Like All Of The Rest

Today I'm going out,
Out to meet some boys,
So I have to get ready
While playing my CD that will make a lot of noise.

I don't know what outfit to wear
Because I have extremely lots,
Shall I wear a skirt or shorts?
A top with stripes or spots?

Tights, leggings or leg warmers,
But then what colour will it be?
I think I'm choosing my outfit now
And I think it really suits me.

A pink top and denim shorts,
A white chunky belt and high-heel shoes,
Fluffy pink leg warmers,
That is the outfit that I choose.

Now I've got to do my hair,
Straightened, scrunched or curls.
Down, up, side or behind,
Maybe in thick angel twirls.

That's it, it's final,
Scrunched it will be,
With my side fringe straightened,
As soon as nothing else is going right for me.

Now for the finishing touches,
I 'put on my face',
And if I want to go out on time,
This is a real race.

I apply my foundation,
But in great powdery lumps,
Then stroke on my mascara
In its thick, gooey, black clumps.

I need to put on my blusher
To make my cheeks look more red.
I have to use red eyeliner
Because my pink has run out of lead.

I close my eyes
And put on my eyeshadow, half white and half pink,
It's the first time I've managed to do it,
And it looks great with a wink.

Before putting on lipstick,
I need to polish my teeth,
Then I put on the frost lipstick, then finally
Shine my lips with gloss that shimmers like morning dew on a leaf.

Although outside I am immaculate,
Inside I don't really care,
It's the person within me that matters,
Not my clothes, make-up or hair.

Emily Light (11)
Fort Pitt Grammar School for Girls

Friendship

Friendship is a big sleepover party,
So fun and like a huge, sparkling grin!
Friendship can have ups and downs,
Like a roller coaster!
Friendship can be thrilling, happiness like a
Glowing butterfly fluttering in the summer sky.
Sometimes friendship can feel like
You have been pushed off a London building.
You feel you need a big warm hug from someone special.
A huge hug, as warm as a giant ball of cotton wool.
That's why you need . . .
Friends.

Tiffany Coller (12)
Fort Pitt Grammar School for Girls

Bullying The Puppy!

I can smell
Her coming nearer,
I smell her every day,
That smell just makes
My tail touch the floor and my paws grip tight.

I can hear
Her shouting and screaming.
What have I done?
They thought I was
Cute, sweet, innocent, but not anymore,
I just get in the way.

I can see
Her foot swing back,
I can see it coming closer.
I can't run or hide,
She will get me, she makes me feel small.

I can feel
My bones crack, they're not getting better,
I feel fragile and weak,
I could drop to the floor, lay down and die,
But my life goes on in pain.

I know
One day someone will care,
They will
Love me, cuddle me, but I need to wait until tomorrow
To see what they will do.
Punch, kick or threaten, I don't have a clue.

India Gillan (11)
Fort Pitt Grammar School for Girls

Standing Alone

People stare as I walk past,
People's whispering stops as I walk past,
People's movements freeze as I walk past,
This is the usual day.

My only friend stares and tells me the truth,
My only friend whispers to tell me the truth,
My only friend freezes telling me the truth,
This is the usual day.

People stare as I make another mistake,
People whisper as I make another mistake,
People freeze as I make yet another mistake,
This is the usual day.

People stare as I run out of the door,
People whisper as I run out of the door,
People's movements freeze as I run out of the door,
This is the only way.

I imagine people staring and cry all the night,
I imagine people whispering and cry all the night,
I imagine the people freezing and cry all the night,
My final decision is made.

People stare as I walk past,
People's whispering stops as I walk past,
People's movements freeze as I walk past,
Please go away, I say.

Hannah Stanford (12)
Fort Pitt Grammar School for Girls

Secondary Schools!

Secondary school, I know it's tough,
Just do your work, that's enough!
Pay attention, obey the rules,
That's the guide to secondary schools!

Do your work, don't sit around,
Do it quietly, don't make a sound!
Talk when asked, never shout,
Throw books and you'll be *out!*

Secondary school, I know it's tough,
Just do your work, that's enough!
Pay attention, obey the rules,
That's the guide to secondary schools!

Have all your equipment ready for class,
Don't forget your books or be last!
Be nice to teachers, never moan,
Do your work without a groan!

Secondary school, I know it's tough,
Just do your work, that's enough!
Pay attention, obey the rules,
That's the guide to secondary schools!

Walk in class, never run,
Do the work you think is fun!
Look at the board, hear the pens squeak,
And you'll have fun every week,

Secondary school, I know it's tough,
Just do your work, that's enough!
Pay attention, obey the rules,
That's the guide to secondary schools!

Pay attention, obey the rules,
This is your guide to secondary schools!

Sophie Hatherly (11)
Fort Pitt Grammar School for Girls

Being Different

Everyone looks at me as if I'm an alien,
Nobody wants to be my friend,
I do have a face, two eyes and ears,
But they still stare, even when the day ends.

Even though they all stare at me,
I still want one as a best mate,
Someone who'll laugh and play
And share a double date.

I feel upset when people laugh,
I go to my room and cry.
When kids on my street go out and play,
I'm in my room, swatting a fly.

I wish when people look at me
They wouldn't stare,
I wish they'd look straight at me
And not my chair.

But then again,
I am different, yeah,
But I can't help the fact
That I'm in a wheelchair.

Elizabeth Early (11)
Fort Pitt Grammar School for Girls

Celebrity

All I did was sing a song,
It didn't take that long.
Then it was in the hits,
I was a star like Brad Pitt.

At first it wasn't so bad,
Until I saw this drunken lad.
Then he said my song was rubbish,
It made me feel miserable and grubbish.

I ran to my groovy hotel,
Thinking of my old motel.
Running as fast as I could to my room,
Remembering the poor old man with a broom.

Hoping that he was okay,
On his own shouting, 'Olé.'
He was the man across the landing,
Wherever I looked, he was standing.

I told my mum about this,
Whilst she was reading the magazine 'Bliss'.
She told me he was my grandad,
The humungous bomb had landed.

My life was over being a celebrity,
I don't mind because I'm with my family.

Aimee Martin (11)
Fort Pitt Grammar School for Girls

Back To School

I woke up very early today,
I couldn't get back to sleep.
I wonder if I'll know the way?
Then my alarm clock started to bleep.

I wash and carefully do my hair
And finally dress in the clothes
That have been hanging all holiday there.
I'll look like all the others, I suppose.

I'm nervous, apprehensive,
I check my bag again.
My mum said it was expensive,
But she didn't want to complain.

I don't fancy breakfast,
I'm trying to play it cool,
The clock says it's half-past,
Time to go to my new school.

Rebecca Helm (11)
Fort Pitt Grammar School for Girls

Christmas

C hristmas is a time for celebration,
H appy families to love and cherish,
R emembering the homeless and the poor,
I nteresting presents to open and to wrap,
S tars twinkle upon the moonlit sky,
T ime to share the jubilation,
M erry Christmas and a happy New Year,
A n angel on top of the colourful tree,
S now glistening on the ground.

Karisma Sathi (11)
Fort Pitt Grammar School for Girls

Sharks

As streamlined as a bullet and as fast as a cheetah,
They live in the ocean in the depths,
Or sometimes nearer the surface.
Striking fear through all that see them
As their famous razor-like fin breaks through the surface of the water,
Prehistoric monsters that have been roaming
The Earth for millions of years.
From centimetres long at birth, to
Nine or ten metres long at their prime,
Scars from battles for females and land,
Hunting and fishing lines contribute to more.
They have been hunted for their meat and fins
Over hundreds of years.
They have evolved to perfection over centuries,
Making them one of the world's most vicious predators.
So, man-eating beasts or just misunderstood?

Charlotte Deeley (11)
Fort Pitt Grammar School for Girls

Detentions

Why were detentions ever invented?
Why were detentions ever invented?
I didn't mean it, I only pretended.

Watching the people walk on by,
Watching the people walk on by,
Waiting for the clock to tick on by.

Talking to myself, waiting for time to fly by,
Talking to myself, waiting for time to fly by,
Looking at the teacher watching me with pride.

She's giving me evils while I want to go outside,
She's giving me evils while I want to go outside,
Now I'm scared, as well as petrified.

Guvandeep Dio (12)
Fort Pitt Grammar School for Girls

Out Of The Window

Looking out of the frosty windowpane,
I stare at the busy world.
People walking, plants moving,
The amazing, wonderful world.

A tree swaying in the wind,
Side to side until the wind has died.
Leaves whirling in the air,
The amazing, wonderful world.

Litter travelling along the ground,
Hitting the ankles of unsuspecting people.
The flowers wave to and fro,
The amazing, wonderful world.

I am awoken from my daydream,
Back to unbearable maths.
But I know the world is out there,
The amazing, wonderful world.

Rebecca Harpum (12)
Fort Pitt Grammar School for Girls

Waiting For You

I sit here by the telephone
Waiting for you to call home.
I hear a noise, I look behind,
But is it you I see this time?
No, it's just the doorbell chime.
Well back to waiting for you.
I put the TV on to watch
And I get myself a drink of Scotch.
Nearly nine, I wonder where you are,
I go to get a snack,
Then there is a tap on my back.
I turn around and there you stand.
You say to me,
'Sorry I'm late, time for tea.'

Liberty Duvall (12)
Fort Pitt Grammar School for Girls

Have You Ever?

Have you ever wanted to fly,
Soar right up high to the sky?

Have you ever dreamed of being rich,
Moving out of this awful ditch?

Have you ever had a fight,
Although you were a feather so light?

Have you ever read a book,
Wished you were a character with good looks?

Have you ever told a lie,
A lie so bad you deserved to die?

Have you ever had a regret,
Caught up in an invisible net?

Have you ever felt so sad,
Felt so sad you cried to your dad?

Have you ever wished to be someone else?
Well actually . . . you'd rather be yourself.

Grace Bell (12)
Fort Pitt Grammar School for Girls

A Monstersitter Needed

In the post office this morning,
I saw this funny sign. This is what it read:

'A monstersitter needed,
Only on Saturday nights,
Pay is one pound an hour,
But I will supply the bites.
You've got to be strong minded
As both of them love a good fight,
But at the end of the evening,
You three should be all right!'

Rhiannon Pike (11)
Fort Pitt Grammar School for Girls

The Spooky Mask

I hid under the blanket and covered my head,
I was very scared and had jumped in my bed.
My mum had brought me a mask for trick or treat,
To go with my costume made out of a sheet.
When I put the mask on I felt really weird,
I decided that now it was something I feared.
When I looked in the mirror, it gave me a fright,
The thoughts in my head I couldn't get right.
I hid under the blanket and covered my head,
I was very scared and had jumped in my bed.
I hid the mask, but it scared me all day,
So I told my dad to take it away.
When I got the mask out and put it on,
I began to hear a spooky song.
I tried pulling it off but it wouldn't budge,
Then I began to sink into sludge.
I was under a blanket that covered my head,
I was very scared and woke up in my bed!

Amy Tibbles (11)
Fort Pitt Grammar School for Girls

We're Going To The Fairground

We're going to the fairground today,
We're going there to laugh and play.
On this day when the sky's so blue,
Riding on the merry-go-round, just me and you.

On the roller coaster, way up high,
Thrashing through the air, soaring through the sky,
Howling with laughter everywhere,
People passing, stop and stare.

Looking around, feeling very lost,
When I'm standing in the queue for the candyfloss,
I am so sad that this day has come to an end,
I will never forget the fun with my friend.

Samantha Rankin (12)
Fort Pitt Grammar School for Girls

Come On Dear

The moonlight beams in the midnight sky,
The little black cat says hello and goodbye.
He waits for his mum to say, 'Come on, dear,
Then you won't have any fear.'

He walked in the blackness of the night,
Then he had a little fright.
In the rustle of the leaves, a hedgehog came out,
She said, 'Don't worry, don't scream or shout.'
He waits for his mum to say, 'Come on, dear,
Then you won't have any fear.'

He still walks on in the darkness of the night,
He soon has another fright.
It was his mum! 'Come on, dear,
It's time to have a great big cheer.
Happy Hallowe'en!'

Bethany Cownden (12)
Fort Pitt Grammar School for Girls

A Football Match

It's 3pm and the whistle blows,
Who will win the match? Nobody knows.
Lee calls for the ball to be passed to him,
Then flicks it into the air and onto his chin.
He keeps dribbling the ball doing double time,
'Leave it to me,' he says, 'this goal is mine.'
Lee sidesteps the goalie and lets the ball go,
The ball hits the net, the crowd shouts, 'Goal!'
Another two balls hit the back of the net,
That was enough, but Lee wasn't finished yet.
Lee tackles his opponent, he was practising all night,
Oh, he's pushed him accidentally, has he started a fight?
Four more goals were scored on that day,
Hip hip hooray,
Hip hip hooray.

Rianne Hall (12)
Fort Pitt Grammar School for Girls

Autumn Evening

The autumn leaves fall softly by
And settle lightly on the ground,
While the cool evening breeze which blows them down
Creates a most unearthly sound.
The sun shines through the bare, twiggy trees,
Casting stick-men shadows on the green.
The grass is sparkling with evening dew,
Dampening trousers which had once been clean.

The air is slowly chilling,
Pinkening my cheeks,
While birds are twittering and chirping,
Preparing for winter sleep.
Dogs run and bark,
Playing restlessly till late hours,
While people sit and think to themselves,
Look at beauty's almighty powers!

Helen Kinney (12)
Fort Pitt Grammar School for Girls

Life Without Love

Life without love would be pointless,
There would be no happiness or reason,
There would be empty hearts,
Gaps waiting to be filled.

Life without love would be nothing,
If you've never felt love,
Then what point would there be to live?
Empty hearts, empty lives.

Don't you see,
All around you there are people,
Waiting to be loved,
Have a heart,

Don't let people live their lives without love.

Jessica Jagpal (11)
Fort Pitt Grammar School for Girls

My Tropical Island

My tropical island is great,
The sun stays out all night.
The soft sand sinks between my toes,
Trees sway in the gentle breeze,
It's wonderful! It really is.

The soft and calming noise of the sea,
The taste of the pineapple is amazing,
I stay at the beach all night,
The sun shines brightly.
The heat from the sun is so hot,
It's wonderful! It really is.

The animals from the rainforests
Are colours of the rainbow,
They're the most beautiful creatures on Earth.
It's wonderful! It really is.

Lucy Attwell (11)
Fort Pitt Grammar School for Girls

The Alien From Mars

There once was an alien from Mars
Who had an interest in cars,
Stole someone's van, went round the bend,
Then tried to mend.
There once was an alien from Mars.

There once was an alien from Mars
Who now didn't have an interest in cars.
He took people's brains and kept them in jam jars,
Then went looking for a few drinking bars.
There once was an alien from Mars.

There once was an alien from Mars
Was now bored of collecting people's brains in jam jars,
Wanted to sail the sea,
Went fishing and got fined a fee.
There once was an alien from Mars.

Louise Campbell (11)
Fort Pitt Grammar School for Girls

Young Writers - Away With Words Poems From Kent

Fright Night

I hate it when it's night-time,
Being sent to bed,
With so many things
Going on inside my head.

Now it's ten o'clock,
There is no sound,
Apart from my dog whimpering
In the basement underground.

I go downstairs to check on him,
I have to creep along,
I break into a cold sweat,
Knowing something is wrong.

I heard a cloak swishing around,
With screams inside my head,
I turned around to look at him,
In a moment I was dead.

Helen Day (11)
Fort Pitt Grammar School for Girls

Bang!

Lights flashing,
People screaming,
Sirens wailing,
Fire's coming,
Air is hot.
News reporters,
Bombs going,
Guilty conscience,
Terrible thoughts,
Bang!
It's over.
Done.
The terror has gone.
The explosion has finished.

Abigail Douglas (11)
Fort Pitt Grammar School for Girls

Chocolate, Chocolate

Chocolate, chocolate,
I want some,
When I eat it I say, 'Yum.'

Chocolate, chocolate,
Brown or white,
I don't care, just take a bite.

Chocolate, chocolate,
Dirty face,
Don't I look a big disgrace?

Chocolate, chocolate,
Big mistake,
This chocolate is so fake.

Chocolate, chocolate,
Makes you fat,
25% saturated fat.

Chocolate, chocolate,
Yum, yum, yum,
Wow! Look at that girl's big fat bum.

Chocolate, chocolate,
Too much for her,
Can I have some please, Sir?

Chocolate, chocolate,
Some for Kim,
Also some for my dog, Jim.

Chocolate, chocolate,
Shed a tear,
Come on! Get your head in gear.

Chocolate, chocolate,
I want some,
When I eat it, I say, 'Yum.'

Cloe Jolley (12)
Fort Pitt Grammar School for Girls

Sasha!

I used to live alone,
With just my mum and dad,
And then guess what?
My sister was born.

My dad drove to the hospital
To see the newborn baby,
My mum let me name her
And it took a little while,
But eventually I said, *'Sasha!'*

We took her home
And let my mum rest,
While I sat with Sasha on my lap.
My mum went to sleep
And so did the baby
And my dad did the washing up.
My mum woke up,
Sasha started crying
And there was no more peace and quiet.
My mum fed Sasha
To make her stop crying.
And that was the best part!

When Sasha turned five,
Guess what she figured?
She figured out how to annoy me.
She went through my room
And broke my stuff,
And my mum said she just wanted to play.

I didn't care what my mum said,
I carried on being annoyed,
Right up until now.
And I still get annoyed by Sasha!

Louise O'Leary (11)
Fort Pitt Grammar School for Girls

PS, I Love You

I read his texts over and over,
Picturing him sitting on his bed,
That's all that's left, memories.
PS, I love you.

If I knew what was coming next,
That last intense kiss would never have ended.
I can't believe it was left that way.
PS, I love you.

He's gone for good, how could it be?
I call his phone
To listen to his soothing voice.
PS, I love you.

Here I am standing over his grave,
This is how I'll seek his love.
I miss him too much. Come back to me.
PS, I love you.

Emily Heasman (12)
Fort Pitt Grammar School for Girls

Hallowe'en

Hallowe'en is finally here,
So let's all make a silent cheer.
Hallowe'en is my worst fear.
When everything goes silent
And I hear a big *bang!*
What is it? What is it? I think to myself.
Could it be my mental health?
Please tell me I'll be all right Mummy,
That there is nothing to hurt me.

Hallowe'en is finally here,
So let's all make a silent cheer.
Kids are trick or treating everywhere,
Suddenly I get a scare.
All along, it was my teddy bear.

Kellie Gadd (11)
Fort Pitt Grammar School for Girls

Taking A Flight

I fly up high, up in the sky,
I look down on the busy world.
Why can't they be with me?
Why can't they be free with me?

I am a bird but they are not,
I feel so lonely, unlike them.
Why can't they be with me?
Why can't they be free with me?

I pray for company, I pray for them all,
I want to be happy along with them.
Why can't they be with me?
Why can't they be free with me?

I'm lonely no more, I'm lonely no more,
There's hope for me now.
They are with me,
They are free with me,
I'm a bird no more, I'm a human again.

Linda Hammoum (13)
Fort Pitt Grammar School for Girls

Cats

Cats are cool, clever and fun,
They love to play and run!
They chase mice
And play with woodlice!

Cats will run after balls,
But never come when they are called.
They will run along the floor
Until they bang into the door!

Chelsea Arnold (11)
Fort Pitt Grammar School for Girls

Outside My Window

I look outside my window
And think of what I see,
A smile to brighten any day,
A little child looking at me.

Her eyes sparkle with stars of joy,
A beauty to compare,
With hair in curly golden locks,
And ribbons in her hair.

She skips along with bounds and leaps,
But wait, she disappears,
Then I hear a roar of laughter
And there, she reappears.

I turn around for one second
And turn to see she's vanished.
This time I hear no voice of happiness,
The daughter of bliss has banished.

A tear runs down my powdered cheek,
For this I don't know why.
I hardly knew this little girl
But already she's said goodbye.

Gabriella Bossman (13)
Fort Pitt Grammar School for Girls

Francesca!

F ull of life,
R unning wild!
A dmires her mum as a superstar.
N ever says yes,
C urly hair,
E ver-changing,
S illy all over!
C uriosity is the key!
A nd all things good!

Naomi Latham (11)
Fort Pitt Grammar School for Girls

Stars In Space

Looking up to the sky,
Wondering what is up there,
All I see is twinkling lights,
But I can't help but stare.

Why are they so bright?
Why do they shine so much?
I wonder if I got close,
I could really almost touch?

Will they ever fall
Right down to the ground?
I might just give them a call
To come see me in my room.

Each and every little star
Will one day be here with me,
As I sit at my bedroom window,
Waiting for a star to visit me.

I wait here by my window as I grow old
And think of this little star,
Lonely and little, all by itself,
Came to visit me.

Sian Varrall (12)
Fort Pitt Grammar School for Girls

Hallowe'en!

Hallowe'en is very close,
So watch out for that eerie ghost.
Vampires, bats, werewolves too,
Are all coming after you.
Mummies and zombies in their tombs,
As screams and screeches fill bedrooms.
Hallowe'en is very close,
So watch out, they're coming to get *you!*

Soriah Williams (11)
Fort Pitt Grammar School for Girls

Football Crazy!

Sitting near the football pitch,
Hearing the crowd's loud cheers,
Hearing all the kicking
Waiting for our ice-cold beers.

Biting our nails looking at the score,
Thinking if there is ever a hope,
Looking at the subs coming out of the door,
With all the crowd trying to cope.

Listening to everybody swear,
While the ref gives a yellow card,
Wondering if they have a care,
Thinking he's being too hard.

Sixty minutes have already passed,
The score being a shameful 2-1,
Hoping that more goals will be cast,
Thinking they are football dumb.

Daisy Counsell (12)
Fort Pitt Grammar School for Girls

Hallowe'en

H allowe'en is here,
A ll give a cheer.
L onely rooms and
L onely souls . . .
O ld skulls!
W ind blowing everywhere,
E veryone has a scare.
E ventually everyone dies,
N ever mind . . . but happy Hallowe'en.

Rosie Jarvis (11)
Fort Pitt Grammar School for Girls

Alone In The Dark

Alone in the dark,
Scared to death,
Wish someone was with me,
Someone to be near me.

Maybe if I looked,
A little person will appear,
I know I shouldn't have,
But I didn't really have a choice.

Escaping from school,
Why did I ever do it?
Something has always been on my mind,
But I have never let anyone know.

All I have ever wanted
Is to have a proper hiding place.
Now I have what I want,
I wish I had told them no to their face.

Aimee Mills (12)
Fort Pitt Grammar School for Girls

Hallowe'en!

Hallowe'en is very near,
So watch out behind your rear.
Ghosts and ghoulies and things that howl,
Werewolves that are on the prowl.
Vampire bats flying through the night,
As on my house shines the moonlight.

Hallowe'en is very near,
So watch out behind your rear.
Orange pumpkins with big round eyes,
Mirror reflections taken by surprise.
Witches and wizards flying through the air,
As monsters are lurking in their lair.

Emily Martin (11)
Fort Pitt Grammar School for Girls

Colours

White is blank and colourless,
It gives me a chill and makes me go stiff.
But if this colour is so boring,
Then why has everybody heard of it?

Oh yellow is so peaceful,
Luminous and happy.
It makes sunflowers look cheerful and lovely,
Like the gold on my earrings gleaming at the sun!

I wonder why Cancer Research is pink?
Maybe because pretty and love are linked?
This colour reminds me of little piglets,
Or when I was little and played with Barbie.

The blood is dripping off the letter 'R',
The deadly rubies round her neck had fire gleaming in them.
Her lipstick was as red as roses
And it was like blood leaking into a field of poppies.

Her eyes were big blue swimming pools,
Gleaming like the sea with raindrops dripping.
There isn't a single fluffy cloud within a powder-blue sky,
But when I see this colour I feel cold and unhappy.

The green, green grass was dripping with envy
As the field next was emerald.
Trees, leaves and stalks were as like in midsummer.
My emerald ring was making everybody's face
Turn green with jealousy.
And now everybody is resentful because they want what I need.

Jordan Turner (12)
Fort Pitt Grammar School for Girls

Seasons

Winter is here,
Snow falling as light as a feather,
Floating down towards the ground,
Laying on top of each other, forming a white blanket.
Icicles dripping from trees,
Splashing onto the ground,
Water droplets joining together to form a sheet of ice.

Spring is here,
Leaves growing as slowly as a snail,
Stretching out towards the early sun,
Grouping together, forming a fresh new tree.
Baby animals running around a field,
Squashing the fresh green grass,
Running together, forming a new group of animals.

Summer is here,
Sun shining as bright as a torch,
Beaming down on the earth,
Shining brightly, forming a brand new day.
Flowers making food for bees,
Opening to let the bees in,
Bees working together to make sweet, sticky honey.

Autumn is here,
Leaves falling as softly as a feather,
Falling towards the ground,
Crumpling together, sounding like crackling fireworks.
Hedgehogs walking to find shelter,
Spikes in the air,
Hedgehogs grouping together to hibernate.

Kelsey Honess (12)
Fort Pitt Grammar School for Girls

The Day The Aliens Came

It had been a very strange day,
Nobody came out to play,
The day the aliens came.

The night's sky clear
And their presence near,
The day the aliens came.

A high-pitched sound,
Near and around,
The day the aliens came.

Brightest light
Came into sight,
The day the aliens came.

Great big blip
Came from a ship
The day the aliens came.

An amazing crash
Carried a clunk and a smash,
The day the aliens came.

'Leave me alone
And you'll stay unknown,'
Is what I said when the aliens came.

Shannon Arnold (11)
Fort Pitt Grammar School for Girls

Living Away From Lies

I need to escape,
Escape from your lies,
Your lying face.

You go and judge me,
I'll tell you what I think
And then you'll judge me again.
You're prejudiced and thick.

Perhaps I like music,
It doesn't make me bad,
When you think 'pop', it drives me mad.

Just because I have friends,
It doesn't make us junkies.
I drive them mad.
But still they love me.

Give me a break
From your speech of power,
I'm not going to be a withering flower.

I've got an open mind,
I know more than you.
I've lived a real life.
What about you?

Sahel Athari (13)
Fort Pitt Grammar School for Girls

The Haunted House Down Our Street

The haunted house down our street,
Of course I never plan to meet,
But after one terrifying dare,
It really did give me a scare.

I entered the house, I don't know why,
At midnight with a pitch-black sky.
I walked up the path as the wind howled,
Nervous as it loudly growled.

Inside was lit by a flickering candle,
Open the doors with a cold, rusty handle.
A whirling wind travelled through the house,
What scuttled by was a diseased little mouse.

I wandered up the creaky stairs,
Across the room flew a battered chair!
I ran back down and didn't look back,
Only to hear a mighty crack.

The haunted house down our street,
Of course I never plan to meet,
But after one terrifying dare,
It really did give me a scare.

Megan Beard (11)
Fort Pitt Grammar School for Girls

Brother Madness

Wake up in the morning
With screaming in your ear.
Who is it, I wonder?
As I look around with fear!

Pulling all the plugs out,
With my TV on and off.
'Who is it?' I bellow.
Then I hear a little cough.

Then I hear some footsteps,
He comes in with a hose!
It's my little brother,
Then he squirts me on the toes!

Then in comes my mother
With her hair like a sheep,
Finally she takes him
And then puts him off to sleep.

Paige Varrall (11)
Fort Pitt Grammar School for Girls

My Meal

I've eaten every scrap of food
That Mum put in my dish,
That's baked beans and potatoes,
And sausages and fish.

I also had some mushrooms
And devoured a tin of corn,
Two chicken legs, four carrot sticks
And one giant king prawn.

If I just ate one more thing
My tummy really would hurt,
Unless, of course, you're offering
To make me some dessert!

Eleanor Camber (12)
Fort Pitt Grammar School for Girls

Recipe For A Perfect Website

To make a perfect website,
There's something you should know,
A graphics site or personal one,
There's a big fat recipe for you to know.

You need:
Blends and brushes,
Knick-knacks,
Scrollbars and backgrounds too,

Though don't use too much glitter,
But add some cute pics,
Put some competitions on
To make it more fun.

Never use your full name
Or your address,
Also keep your email safe,
There's lots of weirdos about!

Keep safe
And you will be fine,
Though also ask your mum and dad
So they know what you're doing.

Natasha Scanlon (11)
Fort Pitt Grammar School for Girls

Ghosts and Ghoulies

H anging lanterns,
A pples, jelly and doughnuts,
L ooming shadows,
L ight and bright colours,
O ranges and fruit not allowed,
W itches and wizards,
E vil lurks round the corner,
E ating sweets all night,
N ever going to run out of sweets.

Hannah Goldsmith (11)
Fort Pitt Grammar School for Girls

Alice On The Phone

A phone call with Alice
L ike a roaring in my ear,
I can't fit in a single word,
C alling, she shouts,
E mily, are you listening?

O n she goes, keeps on yapping,
N othing new to chat about.

T here's moaning at Benj. 'I
H ate him,' she says.
E choing from the TV.

P aper scrunching, I
H ang up.
O h
N o,
E mily.

Emily McCaw (11)
Fort Pitt Grammar School for Girls

Hallowe'en

H orrid vampires,
A mazingly weird pumpkins,
L ooming shadows,
L ight is impossible, dark is the way.
O ver the moon you see a wolf's shadow,
W e enjoy trick or treating,
E vil eyes stare,
E very year we celebrate this.
N asty night skies.

Amber Wright (11)
Fort Pitt Grammar School for Girls

My Family

In my family
I have a sister called Kimberley,
There's a dad called Steve
And he likes to achieve.
I have a mum called Debbie
And she's very steady.
I have a dog called Jasper
Which looks like Casper.
I have a nan
And she likes her pan.
I have an auntie, Sandra,
Who wanted to be called Cassandra.
I have an uncle
Who liked to bunk all.
I have a cousin, Grace,
Who doesn't win a race.
I have a cousin Joe,
Who liked to watch Po.
I have an auntie Lisa,
Who likes to eat pizza.
I have an auntie, Mandy,
Who feels a bit sandy,
I have a cousin Sam,
Who likes to eat jam.
I have an auntie Mary,
Who looks a bit scary.
I have an uncle, Chris,
Who thinks he's all bliss.
He had a dog called Bar Bar,
Who liked to watch Laa Laa.

Lyndsey Piper (11)
Fort Pitt Grammar School for Girls

Guess Who?

Hair lover,
Eavesdropper,
Fashion freak,
Bubble popper.

Remote snatcher,
Fight starter,
Bad catcher.

Loud shouter,
Miss T
Poor singer
A wannabe

Good dancer,
Quick thinking,
Sweet sharer,
Sometimes giving.

Nice at times,
Kind-hearted,
Really pretty,
A few times parted.

Very helpful,
Sticks up for me,
Secret sharer,
Always makes me tea.

Can you guess who she is?
My big sister.

Ore Soyinka (11)
Fort Pitt Grammar School for Girls

Pearl Upon The Sea

The sea is a gentle pearl
And I live among the shimmering grey oysters
In the salty sea beneath the coral,
And so this is my delightful home.

I am a metallic cream and elegant pearl, as my friends have said,
I dazzle in my kingdom beneath the ocean's bed,
And before me are blue and green, different tones,
And so this is my comforting, graceful home.

My friends are the seaweed
And the crashing waves are my whisper when I am alone,
The seashells are my family
And so this is my delightful home.

Safe in my sparkling oyster shell,
Dreaming of the sunlight twinkling upon me,
The stunning anemone surrounded by the dancing clowns,
And so this is my beautiful home.

Paige Arnold (13)
Fort Pitt Grammar School for Girls

Our World

Give your rubbish a fling
And throw it in the recycling bin.
Ice-caps are going,
More rubbish is flowing,
Buildings are destroyed, ash covers the ground,
Harmful gases harm all around,
Lots of bad fumes everywhere,
I hope this poem makes you care.

Anna Saffery (11)
Fort Pitt Grammar School for Girls

Haunted House

It was a dark and stormy night.
If you read this poem you'll be in for a fright.
If you stay in the haunted house,
You might get scared by the shadow of a mouse.

The winds howl, the door creaks,
You might get scared and have a peek.
You look round the door,
But all you see is an apple core.

As soon as you turn round,
You feel a shake from the ground.
A frightening black bat
Comes past you as you see a witch's cat.

You see a frightening ghost come near,
Your spine will tingle with fear.
You run and run and run,
And the vampires cackle, 'It's only a bit of fun.'

If you stay in the haunted house,
You might get scared by the shadow of a mouse.

Caroline Prentice (11)
Fort Pitt Grammar School for Girls

On The Beach

The beach is such a beautiful place,
It puts a smile on everyone's face.

Sand and pebbles on the land,
And crashing waves like a water band.

There's seagulls swooping in the air,
Like they really have no care.

The colour of the sea is blue and green,
That's if the water's really clean.

The tide is now coming in,
So the beach is now a water bin.

Hayley Bowes (11)
Fort Pitt Grammar School for Girls

Night-Time Wonders

In the darkness of the night
I hear birds screech from the trees,
People talking in the street,
Now would you be quiet please?

In the darkness of the night,
Cars speed past in a rush,
Making poor stray kittens squeal,
Now please can you hush!

In the darkness of the night,
Dogs bark madly from the balconies above.
I'm still cold, even though my duvet's wrapped round me.
All I can do is squeeze my white dove.

In the darkness of this night,
Mum comes up to say goodnight,
Pokes her head around the door,
But I'm fast asleep on the floor.

April Taylor (11)
Fort Pitt Grammar School for Girls

Hallowe'en

H ere I am, tucked up in bed,
A ll scared and shivery,
L ying here on this
L umpy mattress I sleep
O n every night, but not tonight . . .
W ho's there?
E ven though I'm
'E re tucked up in bed, I'm scared.
N ow it's morning. The noise was just my teddy.

Stacey Owens (11)
Fort Pitt Grammar School for Girls

Don't Open The Wardrobe Door!

Don't open the wardrobe door
'Cause if you do, you'll get a surprise!
Mum and Dad say there's nothing there,
But you know they're telling lies!

So don't open the wardrobe door,
Please, just leave it alone!
We know there's something in there
And we know you're accident prone!

There's a monster inside the wardrobe,
All grizzly and gruff!
He's plotting something, I tell you,
While he lurks behind your stuff!

I told you not to open the wardrobe door,
And what exactly did you do?
You walked over and you opened it
And it grabbed you and pulled you through!

Now you're a monster, just like him,
Lurking behind the wardrobe door!
I knew you should have listened to me,
And I knew that for sure.

Emma Webster (12)
Fort Pitt Grammar School for Girls

It's Hallowe'en Night

Creak, there's something prowling.
Creak, there's something around.
Creak, there's something lurking.
It's Hallowe'en night, so don't be scared!
Howl, what was that?
Howl, who was that?
Howl, where was that?
It's Hallowe'en night, so don't be scared!

Brontie Stears (11)
Fort Pitt Grammar School for Girls

The Hinkle-Pinkle Monster

I once saw a creature
That was blue, green and red,
And its one time main feature
Was the horn on top of its head.

It had about ten dozen eyes
And lived under the bed.
It told about a thousand lies
And this is what it said:

'I'm the Hinkle-Pinkle monster
Living under your bed.
I go around and scream and shout
Until you're surely dead!'

At this point I ran out of the room,
Out of the house and into the street.
Then I heard a mighty boom
And ran into some hairy feet.

'You can't run away from me,
I'll find you anyway.
I'll use my special powers
To blow you 'til next May!'

I woke up, it was all a dream.
I looked under my bed
Then I gave a massive scream,
I saw that horn on top of its head.

Melanie Jones (12)
Fort Pitt Grammar School for Girls

White Is . . .

White is the snow
That falls when it's cold.
You always know it's there
As it's bright and bold.

White is the moon
That floats in space,
It circles the Earth
At the same pace.

White is the colour
Of a big polar bear,
And the clothes in my drawer
That I wear.

White is food,
White buttons, white mice,
The food I had for dinner,
I had white rice.

White is at school,
The paper and whiteboards,
It is also the colour
Of the milk I poured.

What would the world be
Without the colour white?
Would all these things
Still be in my sight?

Angela Wright (12)
Fort Pitt Grammar School for Girls

Haunted Hallowe'en

Lantern burning light,
Still the moon keeps shining bright,
Darkness comes to make it night,
Children give a fright.

Witches fly across the sky,
On a broomstick up, up high.
Black cat flying with the witch,
Wizard's wand beginning to twitch.

Trick or treaters playing tricks
On those who didn't give them sweets.
Everyone is very scared,
The pumpkin has an evil glare.

Evil spirits fill the streets with bones,
The skeletons are in town!
Ghosts keep the children awake,
Bats fly back to their cave.

Simran Kaur (11)
Fort Pitt Grammar School for Girls

Hallowe'en Scares Me!

H allowe'en always scares me,
A rgh! What was that?
L ove the sweets that I get though!
L iam, my little brother, always plays tricks on me!
O uch! What was that?
W hat's happening to me?
E ek! *Liam!*
E very Hallowe'en scares me.
N ight-time on Hallowe'en scares me more!

Stacey Williams (11)
Fort Pitt Grammar School for Girls

The Dream

As I close my eyes
And begin to doze,
The sun goes down
And the moon, it glows.

As I close my eyes
And begin to sleep,
I think of my dreams
I'll have to keep.

As I close my eyes
And begin to worry
About the sounds of the night
And those creatures that scurry.

As I open my eyes
And begin to wake,
I think of the next night
And the stories I'll make.

Hannah Winterman (11)
Fort Pitt Grammar School for Girls

Hallowe'en!

Hallowe'en is very near,
Hallowe'en happens every year.
Ghosts and goblins can't wait 'til they can pounce,
Children are scared to leave their house.

Hallowe'en is very near,
Hallowe'en happens every year.
Vampires seeking to suck your blood,
Everyone can hear that great thud.
Watch out and beware,
As Hallowe'en is almost here.

Rebecca Ansell (12)
Fort Pitt Grammar School for Girls

Colours Everywhere

Colours everywhere,
Different meanings to me.
White, so popular and fresh,
Orange, hot flames rising,
Yellow, bright and sunny,
Blue, pure like the sea,
Red, bold with love,
Green, calm like grass,
Black, dark with fright,
Pink, so feminine as it fills rooms.
Green and blue, my favourite colours.
Green, so calm,
Blue, so pure.
This the world, sea and land,
But without my yellow, sunny and bright.
My favourite colours would be out of sight,
Nothing but plain black and white.
How could I forget my beloved red?
Red is close to my heart and filled with love.
Colours are important to me,
Making up my wonderful world and life.
Think about colours and you.
What do they mean to you?

Amie Turner (12)
Fort Pitt Grammar School for Girls

What Will It Be Like?

What will life be like in a few years?
Will it be good, or will I shed tears?

What will happen when I am 33?
Maybe nothing, maybe plenty.
Will I be rich and up with the stars,
Or will I just be able to afford a Mars?

What will it be like when I am 58?
Will I be boss, or will I be bait?
Will I be fast and win the race
Or will I stop and go red in the face?

What will I be like at 74?
Will I be fun, or a bore?
Will I be popular with all,
Or will people think I am a fool?

What will I be like at 91?
Will I still be able to run?
Will I be able to dance and shout,
Or will I just be left out?

Will I live to 110?
Will I be as old and rusty as Big Ben?
What will life be like in a few years?
Will it be good, or will I shed tears?

Katie Gray (12)
Fort Pitt Grammar School for Girls

Poverty

Is the death of thousands of people
Not enough to wake us up,
To make us realise we are the only hope?
Saviours of so many, but we're just so selfish.
Our own human life form and we forget about them!
How? Why?

We take forever. We are slow, lazy humans,
So ignorant, so wrapped up in our own little world
We don't realise. We just don't realise.
Our hearts are bleeding with selfishness
As death penetrates others' across the poor parts of the world.

So many poor, dying souls out there,
But so little help.
We talk about how we can change their lives,
Great speeches in front of the EU.
Great big plans, big ideas, loads of talks,
But how is this helping? Ideas are in the mind.
They can't help unless they are truly used,
But most of the time they're not.

Millions of spare pounds pile up in every country
Apart from those poverty-stricken.
But instead of using them wisely to
Help those that are dying, we hold onto them,
Like a protective pack of wolves.

If everyone really cares about those who die
Cold, lonely deaths, then why don't we use our ideas and
Turn our speeches into actions and
Make an impression on those who need it?

Louise Hughes (12)
Fort Pitt Grammar School for Girls

The Celebrity Function

It's the big party tonight,
Celebrities are going to be there all right.
Here comes Paris Hilton holding her cat,
I can't believe Elton John came looking like that!

Keira Knightley is strutting her stuff down the red carpet runway,
Here comes Johnny Depp shouting, 'Yo, ho, yo, ho, bombs away!'
Olivia Newton-John is escorted down the red carpet by
                                        John Travolta,
Posh and Becks couldn't make it tonight, they're on holiday in Malta.

Tom Cruise is looking mighty small,
Rupert Everett is looking gigantically tall.
It's the one and only Dustin Hoffman,
R Kelly is drinking his black coffee can.

Who's this coming down? It's Cilla Black.
Sharon Osbourne is marching down the carpet in her orange mac.
The lovely Duff sisters have arrived,
Rihanna did not just fall, she dived.

Gordon Ramsey is here
To get the kitchen clear.
Debra Stephenson is skipping down the aisle,
Ross Kemp is coming, holding Debra's telephone dial.

Last of all, but not least, Shane Ward,
Then there's me, driving in my new Ford.
This is the celebrity bash,
Now I am going to the bank to get my cash.

Rebecca Cutting (11)
Fort Pitt Grammar School for Girls

I Survived A Hurricane

I stare out into the evening,
I see the grey swirling in the distance,
The clouds erupting around this doom,
Life seems to have disappeared.

I look around and no one's there.
The sense of terror fills the air.
This nightmare edges closer,
Destroying, killing.

It edges closer still,
I have nowhere to run.
My faith has gone, my hope has flown,
I face this murdering vortex.

Its darkness closes over me,
I scream, but sound has gone.
The world is spinning around and around,
Out of control again.

This phenomena, this dream,
Is tearing me and my life apart,
Nothing seems real anymore.
The world's gone black.

I can't move,
I can't see,
I can't hear.
Where am I?

The bright lights,
The quiet buzz of a machine,
Beep, beep, beep.
I open my eyes,
And I'm alive.

I survived a hurricane.

Emily-Jayne Ogley (12)
Fort Pitt Grammar School for Girls

The Peak Of Love

Love is like a mountain
High in the sky.
It took hard work to get there,
But time flew by.
Every now and then it has its little flaws,
An avalanche or two,
But with it built up so strong,
The wind blew it through.

However a mountain has its dangers,
Many, as a fact.
Its vertical cliffs, rocks and sharp points,
But is it an act?
Their beauty is uncovered
When you get to know it.
Was it just a cover up? Safety precaution?
The truth's out, bit by bit.

But love is like a mountain,
An unconditional love.

Kailey Hazeldene (12)
Fort Pitt Grammar School for Girls

Love

Love is an onion!
Strong flavoured and spicy,
Heart-breaking and eye-watering,
Shaped like an opening rose,
Layers of painful red petals
Stinging your heartbroken soul,
Weakening your knees and fluttering your eyelashes,
Tough on the outside,
But all slushy and soft inside.
Your life is now a romantic drama, a roller coaster,
With emotional ups and downs.

Daisy Wellings (11)
Fort Pitt Grammar School for Girls

Dogs

Dogs, dogs, dogs,
White ones,
Brown ones,
Black ones,
Beige ones,
Golden ones,
So many different colours.

Dogs, dogs, dogs,
Labradors,
Westies,
Poodles,
Border collies,
Sausage dogs too,
There are so many different types.

Dogs, dogs, dogs,
Playful ones,
Relaxed ones,
Mischievous ones,
Shy ones,
Loud ones,
Quiet ones,
Small ones,
Big ones,
So many different kinds.

Sarah Allen (11)
Fort Pitt Grammar School for Girls

What Was It All For?

You were wonderful
And good at art,
You made me smile
And filled my heart.

With your care,
You dried my tears,
You made me laugh
And took my fears.

All your passion
Lit a fire
In my soul
With warm desire.

You were all that I dreamt of,
And much, much more,
But you broke my heart,
So . . .
What was it all for?

Isabella Robinson (12)
Fort Pitt Grammar School for Girls

Hallows Eve

H owling in the moonlight,
A t midnight strike the deadly chimes,
L onely in the street,
L onging to go home,
O n and on the trickling of blood goes,
W itches and warlocks roaming the sky.
S hadows upon the ground.

E choes whisper in the cemetery,
V ultures swarm the sky,
E arly morning they disappear, waiting for next year.

Danielle Oliver (12)
Fort Pitt Grammar School for Girls

Will Anything Be Left When I Grow Up?

Will anything be left when I grow up?
Will the grass, trees and flowers still be on the Earth?
Will the sea still be blue?
Will the clouds stay white?

Will anything be left when I grow up?
Will Antarctica stay the same?
Will the endangered become extinct?
Will the sky turn grey?

Will anything be left when I grow up?
Will we be underwater from the rising sea levels?
Will the Africans die of starvation and poverty?
Will the sea turn green and murky?

Will anything be left when I grow up?
Will we stay alive to see the sun die?
Will the poisonous fumes from factories kill us?
Will the wildlife die?

Will anything be left when I grow up?

Sophie Collins (12)
Fort Pitt Grammar School for Girls

My First Day Of Secondary School

My mum stopped the car at the bottom of the hill,
I got out of the car and stood there still,
Still standing at the bottom of the hill.
I saw my friends, we walked up the hill
And stepped in the gates.
We headed towards the hall to find the rest of our mates.
We sat down in the hall,
They sorted us all.
The rest of the day was fine.
I'd finished my first day and now it was time to go away
Till it was time to come back the next day.

Becky Keefe (12)
Fort Pitt Grammar School for Girls

Me And My Family

M um and Dad are very kind people,
E verybody is always chirpy.

A shley is my brother,
N obody can forget the rest of the family.
D ad works for British Airways.

M um works in a kitchen at Chatham Grammar for Boys,
Y our family is probably as nice as mine.

F riends are quite nice to have,
A pparently I have an imaginary friend,
M y school is really nice.
I n primary school I had a rough time,
L uckily I have some very nice friends.
Y ou would like my family if you met them.

Sophie Everest-Ford (11)
Fort Pitt Grammar School for Girls

One Hallowe'en

Scary ghosts and spirits, noises in the night,
Creaking of the floorboards, oh what a fright!
There are graveyards and skeletons scattered all over,
Whereas kids are having parties and sleepovers.
Pumpkins and decorations, all lit up, and so is the full moon
With werewolves in the background.

Children come knocking on people's doors,
Holding out their little paws and asking,
'Please Sir, can we have some sweets?'
The man replies, 'No you can't! I don't do trick or treats!'
Then sadly off the children go and say,
'Oh dear, we'll have to wait until next year!'
Then they go off and shed their tears . . .

Rebekah Featherstone (11)
Fort Pitt Grammar School for Girls

School . . . At Night

It was cold. Thunder rumbled and lightning flashed.
A wolf howled outside. I walked down the corridor,
The tap in the girls' toilet dripped.
My shoes echoed as I walked on the cold stone floor.
It was dark, I was scared,
And . . . it was Hallowe'en.

Another set of footsteps,
The feeling of eyes upon my back,
I quickened my pace, sped up,
Shadows looming over me, I began to run.
It was dark, I was scared.
And . . . it was Hallowe'en.

Blood on the floor of the school courtyard,
A full moon overhead,
A black cat sat on the wall by the gate,
The footsteps still behind me.
It was dark, I was scared.
And . . . it was Hallowe'en.

Running down the road,
Fearing every corner I approached,
It's deathly quiet.
A wolf howls to the full moon, again and again.
It was dark, I was scared.
And . . . it was Hallowe'en.

I ran the rest of the way,
Through the spooky graveyard,
Up the front path, getting my key I let myself in,
Yell for Mum and Dad.
It was dark, I was scared.
And . . . it was Hallowe'en.

There they are! I see them now!
But why are they on the floor,
Covered in blood?
She's dead, so is he.
It's dark, it's Hallowe'en.
And . . . I'm dead.

Catherine Burrin (11)
Fort Pitt Grammar School for Girls

Abandoned

I'm lost, I'm cold and lonely!
I'm a chicken on the loose.
I miss my cosy bedroom
And my friend, Gerald Goose.

I'm scared of foxes and wolves!
I want to go home.
Even though they dumped me here,
I'm worried on my own.

I'm scared of cars and vans!
I miss my chicken friends.
I want to go home!
When will this nightmare end?

I've woken up, I'm back where I belong,
I've seen my owner.
He says that I just got lost.
Oh! He's such a moaner.

I love my house!
It's warm and snug.
I love my owner,
He gives me a hug.

Apparently I was captured by a fox,
But when I woke up I was lost in the countryside.
From now on, I'm staying in my warm and cosy nest box!

Holly Pearce (11)
Fort Pitt Grammar School for Girls

The First Snow Of Winter

The first snow of winter is like a ballet show.
The dancers prance around everywhere, not knowing where to go!
As the snow softly falls and glistens with brightness,
It stops on the way to give the trees some crystal robes of whiteness!
Beautifully and gracefully it floats through the air,
So when out on your walk, take a moment to care!

Georgette Taylor (12)
Fort Pitt Grammar School for Girls

War World

Hiding in the corner,
I can see through the hay wall,
They're standing outside walking,
Guns dragging along the floor.
Mum and Dad, big sister,
All rounded in a group,
Heads in hands, stand leaning
As they're shouting not to move.
Mum told me to sit quiet,
Whilst sis hid me under the bed,
Said they'll take the young ones,
But they'll take them instead.
One man grabs big sister,
Threatening that he'll shoot.
Sis said, 'I'd rather die
Than give anything to you!'
Now I'm sitting on my own,
Still hiding under the bed,
Not from the men with big guns,
But from Mum, Dad, big sis instead.
I'm just going to wait here,
To wake up to everyone,
Shrieking, shouting, screaming,
But I'm the only one.

Ellouise Martin (13)
Fort Pitt Grammar School for Girls

I Still Love You

I'd wake up to your deep brown eyes
And your thick, dark hair.
You looked so perfect lying still,
What could I do but stare?

But as years went by we grew apart,
There was nothing I could do.
You walked away with another girl
When I'd done so much for you.

You disappeared that hateful day,
You said you needed space.
You looked at me and left me
With a hankie full of lace.

I searched for you and searched for you,
I looked in every bar,
Until I got a text from you,
You were with that girl called 'Char'.

Now two years on, life's not the same,
I cry for you all day.
I have this one last note for you,
I still love you, more than I can say.

Rhiannon Steadman (12)
Fort Pitt Grammar School for Girls

My Dream

My eyes are closing,
I feel so peaceful,
I'm drifting away,
Like a ship sailing far away.

The sun rises up,
It shines down on me,,
Running through the fields
With the wind in my hair.

I skip, I cartwheel,
I dance, I smile,
I lay on my back
And stare at the sky.

When I walk,
I spot an old swing,
My eyes fill with joy
As I run so fast.

I swing my two legs
And after some time,
I'm swinging so high,
I am a bird in the sky!

But then a loud noise
Fills my two ears,
I turn my body
To faintly see the time.

Emma Zakrzewski (13)
Fort Pitt Grammar School for Girls

Hallowe'en

I light my pumpkin on Hallowe'en night,
Lying in my bed so scared,
I try to ignore it.
Bang! 'Argh!' I scream with fright.
I sneak along the corridor,
It's too dark to see.
'Boo!' It was my sister jumping out on me.

Oh I really hate Hallowe'en,
How scared I have been.
I hate Hallowe'en,
Another year to go.

Vampires high up in the sky,
I look out of my window as they zoom by.
The sound of devils
Screeching in my ear,
I am so glad my dog's in here.
I can feel the goosebumps on my legs,
It feels like someone's poked me with pegs.

Oh I really hate Hallowe'en,
How scared I have been.
I hate Hallowe'en,
Another year to go.

Gemma Morgan (11)
Fort Pitt Grammar School for Girls

My First Day At Fort Pitt

My heart beat fast,
I was here at last,
There was no big parade . . .
I was so afraid.

I was lost at first,
Some rooms seemed cursed,
I couldn't find my way -
What a scary day!

I felt like a tiny mouse
In a massive house,
Like a flower in a field,
It didn't seem real!

Luckily I survived that day,
I couldn't believe it, *no way!*
I had so much work to do at home,
On my own at home . . . I felt so alone.

I then went to sleep,
All bundled up like a sheep.
I actually looked forward to the next day,
Because . . . it was school again!

Leigh Hookway (12)
Fort Pitt Grammar School for Girls

Hallowe'en Is Near

Hallowe'en is near so hide away,
Ghosts come out all night, never day.
Their huge ebony eyes scare you to fear,
So just remember, Hallowe'en is near.

Witches' cackles screech the night,
As their bats and cats give you a fright.
Five in the morning, they're still here,
So just remember, Hallowe'en is near.

Mummies' arms walk straight and stiff,
People stare, is it real or a myth?
Their silky bodies light up as they sneer,
So just remember, Hallowe'en is near.

Vampires go on a blood hunt,
Staring at the children they call runts.
Children shaking from windows as they peer,
So just remember, Hallowe'en is near.

So just remember all these haunts,
That when you go to sleep they daunt,
And don't go outside and leer,
Just remember, Hallowe'en is near!

Alyss Chuter (11)
Fort Pitt Grammar School for Girls

Hallowe'en

Blood trickling down the wall,
Pumpkins sitting, looking so tall,
Scary faces frighten me,
Hairy spiders crawling up my knee.

Bats screeching, an awful sound,
Children trick or treating all around.
Sitting on my bed in my devil outfit,
Shaking nervously as I sit.

I felt things under my bed,
So scared, I felt a mess.
Was it my brother scaring me,
Or a real monster that I can't see?

Hallowe'en is so scary,
Makes me go shivery!
My knees are shaky, so hard to control,
I'm getting goosebumps thinking about dead souls!

Werewolves and owls screeching in my ear,
Hallowe'en is my worst fear.

Kerri Willis (11)
Fort Pitt Grammar School for Girls

Family

Banging and roaring around the house,
Charging towards me like raging bulls,
Getting ready . . . waiting, waiting,
Bang! They knock me flying off my feet.
'Had a good day at school? What did you do today?'

My mum, young, pretty and kind,
A bit of a nutter, but I don't mind.
Getting madder every day,
But special to me in every way.

My stepdad, tall, cool and funny,
Looking after me he's as sweet as honey.
Getting sweeter every day,
And special to me in every way.

My big brother, gruesome, teenaged and lazy,
If I borrow his stuff he goes terribly crazy.
Getting lazier every day,
But special to me in every way.

Ashleigh Kavanagh (12)
Fort Pitt Grammar School for Girls

About My Old Dog

Today I'm celebrating the birth of my dear dog,
Though she died one year today.
The whole place felt melancholy, with no dog
To guard our house and to protect us from danger.
Sadie was as quick as lightning; no one could catch her.
We had to tempt her with food, but that stopped working.
She just wouldn't eat.
Slowly, she became a wilted flower.
Cancer!
Cancer is what took her life!
There was no point in letting her suffer.

I shall never forget her.
Sadie is still first in my heart.
Though Sadie has a little rival,
Our new puppy, Skye . . .

Daniella Scowen (11)
Fort Pitt Grammar School for Girls

Love Is In The Air

Love is in the air
When the morning sun rises,
The men get up and run to their wives
With every delight inside them.
The sun falls down,
Drags the love with it,
No love shall be in the air tonight,
But then one small light dot climbs up.
The little creatures on the ground rustle,
All over the ground,
Running and scuttling,
All bumping and tripping over,
But when the sun rises,
All the little insects run
To their wives and sleep
And the men start the day all over again.

Ben Newman (12)
Greenacre School

Death

Bombs, guns, blood and tears,
Bring destruction through the years.
People fighting for love and race,
Missiles blasted from outer space.

All the lives lost and gone,
All from the blast of just one bomb,
Like a harvest throughout the year,
All the lives just disappear.

Families torn apart by war,
Just from one man settling a score.
Some lay there in a hospital bed,
Though some are dead, shot in the head.

It never ends, it never stops,
Out at war, bodies left to rot,
All because of the fatal shot.
At the moment we are at war with Iraq,
But who knows what comes after that?

You'd think we'd know that war's not right,
Sending more men out to fight,
More bombs, more guns, more blood, more tears,
You'd think we'd learn, after all these years.
More lives are lost and we shed more tears.

People may fade away,
But death's one thing that's here to stay.

Jack Brydges (12)
Greenacre School

I See

I see
The birds,
The trees,
I see dogs barking down the road.

I see
Time,
Space,
I see the planets aligning.

I see
The sea,
The fish,
I see the whales jumping out of the water.

I see
Fire,
The lava,
I see the volcano explode into molecules of ash.

I see
The clouds,
The treetops,
I see the birds flying in the sky.

I see
Death,
Life,
I see the black hole disappearing into the Earth.

I see.

Lewis Dunn (12)
Greenacre School

A Poem Describing The Modern World

Sadness,
People taunting,
Calling names.

Plans, bombs,
Secret meetings,
Plots to kill
For what they
Believe in.
Terrorism!

Explosions,
People, death haunts the world,
Everywhere, deserted streets,
The war, the bombs!

Decisions,
Decisions people will regret.
The crowds, the speeches,
The government.

Everywhere,
Deserted, broken,
Destroyed, crumbling,
Hatred is blood being spilt!

Andrew Walters (12)
Greenacre School

Washed Away

Washed away,
One's love,
One's home,
One's life.

Washed away,
One's dreams,
One's fate,
One's destiny.

Washed away
To a better place.

A place of truth,
A place of justice,
A place of happiness.

Not a place of darkness,
Nor a place of crime,
Or of theft.

Wait, what's this?
Shadows emerging
All around me,
Darkness . . .
Swallowing my soul,
My dreams.

No more light,
No more truth,
No justice
Or happiness.

Swallowed for eternity,
Washed into a tomb of darkness,
Where dreams are nightmares.
Fate is gone,
Happiness is now hatred.

Washed away,
Never to come back.

Calvin Dawson (12)
Greenacre School

Confusion Of Love

Those simple words confuse me,
For I thought I knew what they meant,
Until I lost and won some,
My love today is for rent.

I love you.

Those simple words I know so well,
I wish for you to know
That just liking someone is so different,
So I will say it really slow.

I love you.

Those are the words of a million feelings,
My hopes and dreams and joys.
Little girls writing love letters,
Chasing after boys.

I . . . love . . . you.

Those are the words I say to you,
I whisper them to your heart.
You turn and look back at me,
I loved you from the start.

David Vincent (12)
Greenacre School

Destruction of 9/11

Think how many people go to work
One day in New York?
Then unexpectedly one morning,
Two planes shocked the world.
On all TVs the world was watching.
Imagine 2,000 people dying because of two planes.
This was the day that changed the world!
3,000 people were killed because of six men.
Just like that, all gone!

Chris Dyer (12)
Greenacre School

War

Why did I do this?
Why didn't I give my wife one last kiss?

I walked through the training doors,
The sergeant gave me a gun and clothes and said, 'They're yours!'

So all of us went to the front,
I asked the sergeant what it was like and he gave me a grunt.

I was sitting in the trenches, dirty and cold,
There was a man next to me, he was very old.

All of a sudden, I heard the whistle blow,
So I shouted, 'Come on, boys, let's go!'

I saw a gas bomb go off and my mate had a violent fall,
The gas has come to kill us all.

Finally the war has come to an end and all my friends are dead,
As I stood up in the trenches, a sniper shot me in the head.

Joe Bliss (13)
Greenacre School

What We Think About Stars

People think stars are miniature,
But really they are bigger than the sun.
Some think they are sinister,
But studying them can be so much fun.

You cannot see them in the day,
But they shine bright on a clear night.
Our favourite being the Milky Way,
In the night sky it shows so bright.

Scientists gaze through telescopes,
While millions of others just look.
Stars dance across the night sky like antelopes,
But mostly they shimmer and our imagination is took.

Jordi Hawks (11)
Greenacre School

The World Cup

They told us it was our year
And that we had nothing to fear.

We're gonna win the World Cup,
We're gonna lift that trophy up.

Beckham, Gerrard, Terry and co,
Singing the Queen's anthem, standing in a row.

As the whistle's blown, the game begins,
The look on their faces, determined for wins.

Sadly, it was not meant to be,
We were undone by a referee.

It seems to happen every four years,
Every fan is left in tears.

Jake Simmonds (11)
Greenacre School

Bullies

Bullies are cowards,
Hiding behind their mates.

But when they're alone,
They're nothing but wimps.

Some bullies are bullies in hoodies,
Because they think it's cool.

Or others are bullies
Because of problems at home.

But there are people here to help,
Charities, teachers, parents and lots, lots more.

So a message to bullies is, it's not cool,
It doesn't make you look big,
In fact, it makes you look small.

Jake Elliott (11)
Greenacre School

Bullies

Bullies think they are good,
They act the way they think they should.
Don't let the bully get you down,
Next time he decides to have a go,
Just let out a gentle sigh or frown.

Do not give him the benefit of a reaction,
Try to be careful that it does not show,
I know how deep down it hurts you,
But this he must not know.

Remember that he perceives people as a threat,
Fearing that they are more gifted than he,
He feels acutely smaller and insecure
And this is what you must see.

And should it ever seem to you
That this torment will never end,
Just remember that I will be here for you,
Your lifelong friend!

Charlie Anderson (11)
Greenacre School

War Poem

Trenches run red,
The sky is full with blue,
Nothing can bring me back to you.

As I fall into the thick yellow smoke,
I find I am starting to choke.

My lungs are burning,
I am now learning,
I shouldn't have gone back to you.

I'm now gasping for my last breath,
As I soon find my first death.

Michael Willy (13)
Greenacre School

London

London is a busy place,
I walk up and down,
Then I see a beggar,
My face is like a frown.

London is a busy place,
There's so many things to do,
Like going to museums
And visiting the zoo.

London is a busy place,
Buildings big and tall,
Many full of history,
Science, sport and all.

London is a busy place,
With people from all races.
Young and old, brown and white,
All going at different paces.

Michael Jones (11)
Greenacre School

Wedding

(Written for my aunt and uncle's wedding)

Wedding is the occasion,
1 + 1 is the equation,
Love is the root of happiness
And a great sensation.

Love can have its ups,
But have its downs too,
But when you're in love as much as these two,
You stick together like glue.

Now the wedding bells have been rung
And joyous songs have been sung,
We hope you will be
Together forever.

Robert Hill (13)
Greenacre School

My Dreams

I have my dreams,
What do they mean?
Full of hope and joy,
I am a lucky boy.

I see myself in years to come
Achieving all,
Walking tall,
I even get to play football.

I grow into a man,
I have lots of plans.
My life is great,
But I make mistakes.

I remember when I was a boy,
That special, favourite toy,
When life was fun
And Chelsea always won.

I wake to find
It was all in my mind.
I have my dreams,
What do they mean?

Mitchell Goee (12)
Greenacre School

Young Writers Information

We hope you have enjoyed reading this book - and that you will continue to enjoy it in the coming years.

If you like reading and writing poetry drop us a line, or give us a call, and we'll send you a free information pack.

Alternatively if you would like to order further copies of this book or any of our other titles, then please give us a call or log onto our website at www.youngwriters.co.uk

Young Writers Information
Remus House
Coltsfoot Drive
Peterborough
PE2 9JX

(01733) 890066